SONG
OF THE ARAB

by ROLLA FOLEY

The Religious Ceremonies, Shrines and Folk Music
of the Holy Land Christian Arab

THE MACMILLAN COMPANY · NEW YORK · 1953

The New Testament quotations are from the *Revised Standard Version of the Bible*, copyrighted 1946 and 1952 by the Division of Christian Education, National Council of Churches, and used by permission.

FOR FLEUR.

Preface

IT was the author's privilege to live amongst the Holy Land Christian Arab from 1939 to 1945. During this interval he worked amongst a nation of peaceful and happy people, collecting vast amounts of information relating to their folk songs, instruments, costumes, dances, customs, and folklore. For the past nine months the writer revisited the same area to resume his work amongst the Arab neighbor. During his visit a careful check was made of all the hitherto recorded data so that a true perspective of the culture and folkways of the Arab could be presented. That story is related in the chapters that follow.

Song of the Arab is a story that grew out of a vital inner experience with a people whose culture and folkways are an important contribution to our modern world. The core of that culture is presented in such a way that the reader might relive and share in the folkways of the Arab world. The royalties from the sale of this work are being contributed toward the financial assistance of Arab refugee students who are presently studying in American universities under the auspices of the Holy Land Arab Refugee Student Fund.

The author is indebted to many people for their kindness and help in the collection of information and the preparation of the manuscript in its final form.

A special acknowledgment is due to Wadi Mitri Shatara, trusted Arab friend in Ramallah, Jordan, for her kindly and discerning helpfulness in guiding me in the selection of folk tunes and tales of warmly human interest. Anna Rychster-May of Jerusalem, now in her late eighties and almost totally blind, has sketched the line drawings with accuracy and beauty. The maps of the Holy Land, and the musical settings, are the exacting work of Krikor Ulubeyan of Aleppo, Syria. Folk words translated from the original Arabic were carefully checked by Wadi Mitri Shatara. English adaptations were corrected and occasionally improved by Alice Whittier Jones, with the assistance of Alice Perkins. Grateful acknowledgment is extended to Beatrice Krone for her version of "Our Prayer," adapted from the writer's original translation.

An unusual number of friends, many of them Quakers associated with the American Friends Mission in Ramallah, have been most helpful. Alice Whittier Jones, Marion E. Kelsey, and Laura E. Davis have been gracious and untiring in their helpfulness. Ellen Scott, Bert and Iris Riley, Alice Perkins, and Flo Foley have read the completed manuscript and offered invaluable guidance and helpful criticisms. Additional courtesies have been extended by Merle L. Davis and Martha K. Tubesing of the American Friends Board of Missions at Richmond, Indiana, as well as Mildred E. White, principal of the Friends Girls' School at Ramallah.

The governments of the Near East have given the writer complete freedom and enthusiastic encouragement in the pursuit of his project. Special acknowledgment is made to the Jordanian Government—its Foreign Office, Ministry of Education, Department of Antiquities, and the Arab Legion. The Consular Services of the United States of America in Amman and Damascus have been cooperative in every way. Church officials of the various religious orders have been most generous in their interest and help.

Recognition is due to Dr. Max T. Krone, Beatrice Perham Krone, Dr. Charles C. Hirt, Dr. Pauline Alderman, Julia Howell Overshiner, and William Vennard of the University of Southern California at Los Angeles; Mae Nightingale of Le Conte Junior High School of Hollywood; and to Dr. James L. Mursell and Professor Lilla Belle Pitts of Columbia University in New

York City for their combined criticisms, their invaluable encouragement, and continued interest.

Fleur and Madge have been genuinely enthusiastic, encouraging, and at times a bit prodding. Their quiet understanding and
loving inspiration have been of immeasurable help in the joy of
completing *Song of the Arab*.

OAKLAND, ILLINOIS
February, 1953

Contents

Folk Music Illustrated

SONG OF THE ARAB

The Religious Ceremonies, Shrines and Folk Music

of the Holy Land Christian Arab

Introit

THE following treatise is a record of the major religious folk-rites of the Christian Arabs in the Holy Land during the course of a Western calendar year.

The descriptions are based on notes following observation and participation by the writer during a period of nearly seven years in the Near East as missionary, educator, and music consultant. The religious customs, ceremonies, and religious folk music of the Christian Arabs here presented are a sampling intended to make possible a better understanding and a finer appreciation of these people.

This record, combining religious folk music transcribed and compiled by the writer with historical data found in the libraries of the Near East and the United States, will provide the missionaries and the religious and educational leaders of the Near East with heretofore unrecorded material. In spite of necessary restrictions it is the only source book so far available for students of the religious folk music of the Christian Arabs in the Holy Land, and for folklorists and musicologists. The writer hopes that it may stimulate further interest in the recording and use of religious folk music throughout Arab lands.

To understand another race, we must have some knowledge of its geographical location, the topography of its land, its basic racial strains, its contributions to human progress, and its history.

The present-day Arab's interpretation of the Christianity which sprang from the soil of his ancestors cannot be understood without a brief review of the rise and spread of Christianity through his lands, from its birth to its present stature.

Such a résumé should provide the student with an adequate background for the full appreciation of the pageantry, the tradition, and humble sincerity of the folk-rites, the pilgrimages, and the folk expressions of the Holy Land Christian Arab.

CHAPTER I

The Holy Land in 1945

WITHIN the geographical boundaries of the Arab world in 1945 is a modern province called Palestine. In Old Testament days it was part of the country called Canaan. During the Roman rule, at the time of Christ the Messiah, at the time of the Prophet Muhammed, and throughout the Ottoman domination, this stretch of land was a part of ancient Syria. Not until the close of World War I did it gain separate identity and become known as Palestine.

For centuries, however, the area has been regarded as especially hallowed ground by followers of three great monotheistic religions—Judaism, Christianity, and Islam. Today some 770,000,000 world citizens look to this tiny Holy Land as their spiritual home. Of the total, 400,000,000 are Christian and 360,000,000 Muhammedans, while—approximately 6,000,000 Jews having been killed during World War II—only about 10,000,000 people in all profess the Jewish faith.

As the world center of religious attention, Palestine traditionally and annually fosters numerous colorful and ancient religious rites. Pious celebrations the world over have grown from rites first introduced on this sacred ground. From the ceremonies and festivities and from the noble hearts of the people have sprung folk music of melodic beauty and sincerity yet "undiscovered" by the major portion of today's world. From the ceremonies and festivities have grown both simple and elaborate rituals unequaled in guilelessness, supreme devotion, or brilliant pageantry.

In 1942 the population of Palestine was 1,605,816. Of the number 1,114,329 were Arabs, 478,449 were Jews, and the remaining minority were representatives of various other races. The Arab total represented 987,985 Moslems and 126,344 Christians.

We are not dealing here with the Jewish or Moslem populace. Therefore it is well to recognize at once that Palestine is holy land to the followers of Judaism because there Amos, Isaiah, and other Old Testament prophets made great contributions to the spiritual life of mankind. It is holy to the Moslems because Jerusalem was Islam's first Holy City and has been the location of El Aksa Mosque since A.D. 691.

Palestine is a country of only about 10,000 square miles, or the size of the state of Maryland, 47 per cent of it in the ill watered and desert region known as the Beersheba Subdistrict; and other large areas are waterless. It is a part of Greater Syria.

Greater Syria is composed of four separate states: the Syrian Republic and the Lebanese Republic, both declared independent on June 8, 1941; and the Mandated Territories of Palestine and Transjordan. The capitals are at Damascus, Beirut, Jerusalem, and Amman.

Geographic Syria extends from the Taurus Mountains on the Turkish frontier in the north to the Sinai peninsula in the south, and from the Mediterranean on the west to the frontier of Iraq on the east. It is roughly four hundred miles in length and a hundred and fifty miles in width. Its climate is of the Mediterranean type, characterized by rain in winter and drought in summer.

The topography of the land is perhaps unique in combining all conceivable variations—mountains, plains, woods, hills, plateaus, deserts, lakes, rivers and valleys, with the deepest fissure on the surface of the globe, the Dead Sea being about 1,300 feet below sea level. The soil ranges from very fertile in the maritime and inland plains to the arid desert in the east.

The basic racial strain of the Palestinian goes back to the kindred Semitic tribes that abandoned their original desert habitat of the Arabian peninsula and swarmed to the surrounding countries. The peoples of the peninsula subsequently became the Babylonians, the Assyrians, the Phoenicians, and the Hebrews of history. From its sandy soil in medieval times sprung a people who conquered most of the then civilized world, gave the world a new religion—Islam—which still claims the adherence of no fewer than two hundred and forty-six million people, representing nearly all the races. This means that every sixth or seventh person in the world today is a follower of Muhammed.

The basic language of these people is Arabic—a language that is today the medium of daily expression for forty-five million people. For several centuries in the Middle Ages it was the language of learning and culture and progressive thought throughout the civilized world. Between the ninth and the twelfth century more works, philosophical, medical, historical, religious, astronomical, and geographical, were produced in Arabic than in any other tongue.

The Arabs, within a century after their awakening, became the masters of an empire extending from Spain and the shores of the Atlantic Ocean to the confines of China, an empire greater than that of Rome at its zenith. It was not only an empire, but a culture as well. Heirs of the ancient civilization that flourished on the banks of the Tigris and the Euphrates, in the land of the Nile and on the eastern shores of the Mediterranean, they absorbed and assimilated the main features of Greco-Roman culture, and subsequently acted as a medium for transmitting to medieval Europe many intellectual influences which ultimately brought the awakening of the Western world and set it on the road toward its modern renaissance. No people in the Middle Ages contributed to human progress so much as the Arabians and the Arabic-speaking peoples.

The Babylonians, the Hittites, the Phoenicians were, but are no more. The Arabians and the Arabic-speaking peoples were and remain. They stand today, as they stood in the past, in a most strategic geographical position astride one of the great arteries of world trade.

Darkness covered the Arab world when it fell under the sway of the Turks. It did not awaken from its medieval slumber until the nineteenth century, when Western influences combined with a revival of Arabic literature to mark an era of far-reaching national awakening. Nowadays a new spirit stirs the Arab peoples, a spirit destined to carry them along the road of progress and democracy and equip them better to share in advancing the welfare of the human race.

Today Egypt is a sovereign and independent state. Iraq has a king in its capital at Baghdad. Ibn-Sa'ud, the strong man of modern Arabia, has carved and consolidated for himself a large kingdom, including most of central and northwestern Arabia. Syria is a republic. Lebanon is a republic. Transjordan has an amir even though it and Palestine are mandated territories.

From the ancient Arabs, and specifically the Palestinian Christian Arab, this work wishes to record noteworthy details of traditional religious rites, to describe in some detail religious pilgrimages and shrines, and to present a representative selection of religious folk music.

CHAPTER II

The Christian Holy Land

In the thirty-third year of the reign of Herod the Great, a decree from Caesar Augustus ordered the enrollment of all subjects in the land of Syria. "All went to be enrolled, each in his own city." Among those who registered in the city of David, which is called Bethlehem of Judea, were a village carpenter from Nazareth in Galilee named Joseph, "because he was of the house and lineage of David," and his betrothed, Mary, who was "great with child."

While they were there, the time came for her to be delivered. And she gave birth to her first-born son and wrapped him in swaddling cloths, and laid him in a manger, because there was no place for them in the inn.[1]

From this humble birth of a child named Jesus,

nineteen wide centuries have come and gone and today He is the centerpiece of the human race and the leader of the column of progress. . . .

He grew up in an obscure village. He worked in a carpenter shop until he was thirty, and then for three years He was an itinerant preacher. He never wrote a book. He never held an office. He never owned a home. He never had a family. He never went to college. He never put his foot inside a big city. He never traveled two hundred miles from the place where He was born. He never did one of the things that usually accompany greatness. He had no credentials but Himself. He had nothing to do with in this world except the naked power of His divine manhood. While still a young man, the tide of

[1] St. Luke 2:6–7.

7

popular opinion turned against Him. His friends ran away. One of them denied Him. Another betrayed Him. He was turned over to His enemies. He went through the mockery of a trial. He was nailed upon a cross between two thieves. While He was dying, His executioners gambled for the only piece of property He had on earth—and that was His coat. When He was dead He was taken down and laid in a borrowed grave through the pity of a friend.[2]

Yet, from this thirty-three-year-old Nazarene sprang a new religion that today claims as many as four hundred million adherents. The land called Palestine, where he was born and where he lived and taught, is indeed sacred as the spiritual home of a great monotheistic faith. Christians the world over honor and revere the manger of Bethlehem, the home in Nazareth, the Sea of Galilee, the Mount of Olives with its Garden of Gethsemane, and the Hill of Calvary. Cathedrals, temples, churches, and simple sanctuaries have arisen throughout the land made sacred by the life of Jesus and his apostles.

Plebeian and elaborate rites of worship sprang from the sincerity of the early Christians as they devised ways and means of offering homage, thanks, and praise to the Messiah. These sincere efforts of self-expression became traditions. The very traditions took root, sprouted, grew and branched in widely divergent ways, blossoming into the church services and rituals of the present day. The naïve folk songs and chants of the early Christians have sprouted, developed, and branched into every musical sphere—music touching and heartrending in simplicity, or enthralling and awe-inspiring in complexity. No theme has stirred the poets and musicians of the ages into more sublime power of expression than the love of Jesus.

I am far within the mark when I say that all the armies that ever marched, and all the navies that were ever built, and all the parliaments that ever sat, and all the kings that ever reigned, put together

2 James A. Francis, *Behold the Man*. Based on St. John 19:5.

have not affected the life of man upon this earth so powerfully, as has that One Solitary Life.[3]

Lest it be overshadowed in future paragraphs because of the special emphasis being placed in this volume upon customs primarily related to New Testament events, it is well to recognize that, though Christians believe that Palestine was providentially chosen of God to be the scene of the incarnate life of his son Jesus Christ, the New Testament revelation was but the culmination of a long history of a preparatory revelation recorded in the Old Testament. Christians are surely interested in the Holy Land because of its connections with Christ, but also because of its connection with the history of Israel.

[3] *Ibid.*

CHAPTER III

The Rise and Spread of Early Christianity

AMONG Christ's instructions to his disciples were commands to preach and teach. We know that this concern of the Master was fulfilled outright, for Christianity spread rapidly from its homeland, Palestine, into the far corners of the then civilized world.

The new Christian Church, in order to carry on its missionary teachings, soon had to establish convenient geographical centers to provide the ever-growing organization with seats of religious learning, clergy training grounds, and business centers for the carrying on of numerous and necessary activities.

Three Apostolic Churches were soon established with patriarchs leading the bodies of religious leaders or clergy. To St. James is given the credit for the establishment of the Jerusalem Apostolic Church in the capital city of the Holy Land where Christ had so often taught, performed miracles, had been crowned "Hosanna in the Highest," yet crucified and buried, but had risen to be followed and worshiped as "Counsellor," "King of Kings," and "Lord of all."

St. Mark founded the Apostolic Church at Alexandria on the Egyptian shore of the Mediterranean Sea, while Antioch on the Syrian shore became a third seat of learning and guidance.

Early in the Christian Era, persecuted monks fled to Italy to escape imprisonment or death. Naturally a few Christian seeds soon reaped a bountiful harvest which culminated in St. Peter's Apostolic Church in Rome.

In Byzantium (Constantinople, now Istanbul), at the base of

the roaring Bosporus whose waters pour forth from the near-by Black Sea, and on the shores of the Sea of Marmara, one finds the fifth of the centers of Christian gravity.

Jerusalem, Alexandria, Antioch, Rome, and Byzantium, the five great Apostolic Churches, held out a guiding hand to the ever-growing number of Christians, offering them a simple, somewhat rude, but wholly satisfying faith. In general there was oneness in the faith offered by the five reigning patriarchs to their flocks. Naturally the local languages, customs, and manners of these great, far-spread geographical centers were cause for slight deviations in the new faith searching for suitable and effective ways to worship; but until 1050 the cradle of civilization offered one Church, one faith.

In the dark period between the time of the early apostles and the reign of Constantine the Great, the beginnings of most of the practices of the medieval church are to be found. All rites of the early church were based upon Christ's command to "do this in remembrance of me." The music of the period centered around the eucharistic feast, as manuscripts of A.D. 180 prove. These chants were sung by the assembly of worshipers and were accompanied by flutes and wind and stringed instruments.

The Roman Empire reached its greatest expanse and prosperity in the second century. In the third century, symptoms of decay began to appear with Caesar as ruler; but even in the midst of seething, political turmoil Christianity steadily advanced.

A new era in the history of church worship begins in A.D. 306, when Constantine became Emperor of the great Roman world. Pope Sylvester, in A.D. 314, founded a singing school in Rome which is still in existence and is now known as the Sistine Chapel. About the year 325 the religion of Christ became the official or state religion of the Empire. With the edicts of Constantine, which practically made Christianity the dominant religious system of the Empire, the swift dilation of the pent-up energy of the Church inaugurated an era in which ritualistic splendor kept pace with the rapid acquisition of temporal power.

The repeated onset of Goths, Vandals, and Huns finally drove the government from Rome to Byzantium. Constantine the Great ruled until A.D. 333.

In 350 Flavian and Diodorus introduced antiphonal singing into the Apostolic Church at Antioch, thus taking away the major part of the musical service from the worshipers and giving it to a newly developed clergy choir. The clergy were now being ordained for the first time.

Another very important historical event in the history of sacred music was the meeting of the Council of Laodicea, sometime between the years 343 and 381. This official religious gathering gave the world the first law pertaining to church music, in its thirteenth Canon: "Besides the appointed singers, who mount the ambo and sing from the book, others shall not sing in the church." Although to many this act of robbing the worshipers of their privilege of raising their voices in praise to God seems to be a backward step in individual worship, it heightened the importance of music in the worship service.

In the early seventh century two military invasions changed the course of Christianity as a one-Church, one-faith organization. Two distinct church branches, the East and the West, are direct results of the invasions.

From the north of Rome, Teutonic tribes were successful in overthrowing the capital. The invading tribes, all pagan, soon came to accept the Christian faith and gave new life and strength to the Apostolic Church in Rome. Christianity was then propagated into the distant North and West, becoming a mighty social institution.

The new strength and power gave rise to a declaration from Rome that the Roman Catholic Church was henceforth a separate branch of the Church. This pronouncement, which shook and shattered the very foundation upon which the church was built, was made without consulting the government and church in Byzantium. Charlemagne (Emperor Charles I) immediately set about blending the various Roman, Eastern, and Teutonic influences into a formal "style" for the new branch of the Christian Church.

Charlemagne, a mighty warrior and a clever statesman, was also a patron of the arts, learning, and music. Numerous churches and palaces after the Byzantine manner were built at his command, all decorated with ornate mosaics and frescoes. A blend of Northern, Southern, and Eastern characteristics in the art of the time was further intensified by his direct contact with the culture of Italy during his military conquests. Charlemagne ordered the establishment of music training centers in various churches of his empire in order that the music of the Church might be sung according to the best traditions of Rome. The popular songs and hymns of the Franks were collected so that posterity might have a record of the music of his time, but all were destroyed as being too "pagan" at the command of his son and successor, Louis the Pious.

Charlemagne, King of the Franks from 768 to his death in 814, was truly the head and father of the new Roman Catholic Church. Established Church doctrines were revised. Divine power was vested in the Pope. He became a mediator between his subjects and God, and purgatory was introduced as part of the new Church belief.

The Greek language remained for a long time the liturgical language; but the Church finally became Latinized, leaving only one part of the service with a Greek text, the *Kyrie eleison*. So, unlike the Christians of the East who, in practice of their cult, employed many languages, the Christians of the West shared one common language: Latin. The new national elements—Frankish, Celtic, Visigothic, and so forth—present in Rome since the northern invasions, crept into the chant of the West to some degree; but the use of an international tongue presented a counterbalancing element of universality. At first the Roman chant, which was to prove by far the most important influence in the development of Western music and its notation, lagged behind the repertoires produced in the Near East; but the conquests in the Near East were driving many Syrian monks into Italy, and their liturgic practice—half Greek, half Semitic—could not fail to make itself felt among their adopted brethren. Rome, then, became a church-service melting pot which accepted the best from the East, retained the best of its own liturgy which already had a flavoring of Northern paganism, and built up a service that was fresh, virile, and adaptable to the times.

In the reign of Charlemagne the Council of Aachen (held in 803 A.D.) enjoined upon all monasteries the use of the Roman song, and a later capitulary required that the monks should perform this song completely and in proper order at the divine office, in the day-time as well as at night. According to other rescripts during the reign of Louis the Pious, about 820, the monks of St. Gall were required daily to celebrate Mass, and also to perform the service of all the canonical hours. The solemn melodies of the ancient psalmody resounded daily in manifold and precisely ordered responses; at the midnight hour the sound of the *Invitatorium, Venite exultamus Domino,* opened the service of the nocturnal vigils; the prolonged, almost mournful tones of the responses alternated with the intoned recitations of the lessons; in the spaces of the temple on Sundays and festal days, at the close of the nightly worship, there re-echoed the exalted strains of the Ambrosian hymn of praise (*Te Deum laudamus*); at the first dawn of day began the morning adoration, with psalms and antiphons, hymns and prayers; to these succeeded in due order the remaining offices of the diurnal hours. The people were daily invited by the *Introit* to participate in the holy mysteries; they heard in solemn stillness the tones of the *Kyrie* imploring mercy; on festal days they were inspired by the song once sung by the host of angels; after the *Gradual* they heard the melodies of the Sequence which glorified the object of the festival in jubilant choral strains, and afterward the simple recitative tones of the *Creed;* at the *Sanctus* they were summoned to join in the praise of the *Thrice Holy,* and to implore the mercy of the Lamb who taketh away the sins of the world. These were the songs which, about the middle of the ninth century, arose on festal or ferial days in the cloister church of St. Gall. How much store the fathers of this convent set upon beauty and edification in song appears from the old regulations in which distinct pronunciation of words and uniformity of rendering are enjoined, and hastening or dragging the time sharply rebuked.[1]

Until the final cleavage of the Church into its Eastern and Western divisions, the interaction was strong between the two branches, and much of custom and art was common to both. This interchange of ideas so necessary to the preservation of a Church and faith oneness now ceased, from the strain not only of combat resistance against northern invasions in Italy, but of the Arab conquests which demolished the Persian empire and shook the Byzantine power to its very foundation.

By this time Armenia and Persia had well established Christian communities. Missionaries had even penetrated as far as India and the Far East with the message of Love. With the ever steady expansion of the Church, a variety of languages, as Arabic, Armenian, and Syriac, were employed in the worship services. and national elements crept into the liturgies, noticeable in both the poetry and the music. This gave opportunity for more individual self-expression, which at the same time gave rise to new deviations and the establishment of more and more traditions. Along with persecutions by the Orthodox Church, the existence of these new schisms in the Christian Church paved the way for the surprisingly rapid progress of Arabian arms.

Unlike the Teutonic invaders, who strengthened the Roman branch of the Apostolic Church, the Moslem invaders, though extremely tolerant of "nonbelievers" as later paragraphs will show, naturally gained the upper hand and Islam soon became the predominating religion. The majority of the conquered embraced this new religion for the sake of personal safety, perhaps, but more so for social prestige, financial and economic well-being, and general patronage.

Jerusalem, Alexandria, and Antioch ceased to function as cen-

[1] C. Dickinson, *Music in the History of the Western Church,* Charles Scribner's Sons, New York, 1902, pp. 119, 120.

ters of Christian leadership, and Byzantium alone upheld and carried on the traditions that sprang from the womb of Jerusalem. The years 800 through 1054 became, indeed, a dark era for Christianity in the Arab world.

Though Christianity's most prosperous periods in the Near East were between the fourth and seventh centuries and during the Crusades, it is to be remembered that there has been without interruption a Christian community in the Holy Land. Christians, after witnessing centuries of Ottoman neglect, took a new interest in the birthplace of their religion at the beginning of the nineteenth century. Modern schools and hospitals, founded by missionaries representing nearly all branches of the Christian Church, offered effective educational and medical work for all classes of the population with astounding results. Truly the Holy Land witnessed a powerful revival and awakening. World interest is again focused on the earthly home of the King of Kings.

CHAPTER IV

Christianity at Work in 1945

HISTORIANS record that Arabs have lived continuously in the area we now call Palestine more than four thousand years. Only for the past two thousand years, however, have they been the predominating population. In 1918 they constituted 90 per cent of the population; in 1940 they were less than 75 per cent, and by 1942 still less. Official statistics give the population of Palestine at the end of May, 1940, as 1,521,005, of whom 936,896 were Moslems, 453,286 Jews, 118,493 Christians, and 12,330 Samaritans, Bahais, Metawilehs, and so forth. Some of the present Arab population, particularly the Christians among them, are descended from the natives who occupied the country before the days of Abraham. It is on the present Christian population that this writing focuses immediate attention.

We have already noted that Palestine had a Christian-Arab population of 126,344 in 1942. This group quite naturally falls into three categories—followers of the three major limbs that branched from the sturdy trunk of the aged Christian tree.

The Eastern Orthodox Church, which has had a continuous existence in the country since the days of the Apostles, claims 40 per cent of the followers of Christ. Another 5 per cent belong to other national branches of the Eastern Orthodox Church such as the Orthodox Abyssinians and the Copts, both Monophysites, the Armenians and the Assyrians, all with bishops in Jerusalem. These small communities have been in the Holy Land for many centuries. The Roman Catholic Church, including adherents to both Latin rite and Eastern rite, has some 40 per cent of the

Christian population while the remaining 15 per cent belong to innumerable Protestant bodies.

For a full appreciation of the significance and beauty of the traditional religious rites of the Holy Land, it is essential to pause momentarily for a limited examination of the three Christian groups in Palestine today.

THE GREEK ORTHODOX CHURCH

At the head of the Greek Orthodox Church is the Patriarch. His Beatitude Damianos I, raised in 1897, is the present superior. His Beatitude is assisted in the Church government by the Holy Synod, which is composed of fourteen titular Bishops and Metropolitans. The Patriarch is also the leader of the Brotherhood of the Holy Sepulcher. This Patriarchate grew out of the Bishopric of Jerusalem, of which St. James the Less is considered as the first bishop. It is an autocephalous branch of the Holy Orthodox Eastern Church. The Patriarch of Jerusalem became one of the four heads of the Eastern Church after the Council of Nicaea in A.D. 451, when the original Christian Church divided into the Eastern and Western Churches. Since that early date it has been the predominant church in Palestine, except during a century of the Latin Kingdom of Jerusalem at the time of the Crusades, when it was supplanted by the Church of Rome and it occupied a secondary position, the Patriarch residing at Kerak east of the Jordan. It resumed its former position after the capture of the Holy City by Saladin in 1187.

The Patriarchate is wealthy in lands and buildings, both in the holy city of Jerusalem and in the country. It is also wealthy in jewels, gold and silver vessels, and ornaments presented by pilgrims and monarchs in the course of many centuries. It has as many as eighteen convents in various parts of the one city alone, with innumerable institutions scattered throughout the country. Probably the five most important Orthodox spiritual and cultural centers, all in the vicinity of Jerusalem, are the

Monastery of St. Helena and St. Constantine, the Monastery of St. Nicholas, the Monastery of the Cross, and the Monasteries of Gethsemane and Abraham. The Monastery of St. Helena and St. Constantine, together with the Patriarch's house adjoining, is the Greek Orthodox headquarters. This great Greek Monastery was first mentioned in 1400 as the Monastery of St. Thecla. It contains five churches, of which the most important is that of St. Thecla, and a library of valuable ancient books and manuscripts. A flourishing printing establishment is housed in part of the Monastery of St. Nicholas, and a theological seminary of primary importance is included in the Monastery of the Cross.

THE ROMAN CATHOLIC CHURCH

The line of *de facto* Patriarchs of the Roman Catholic Church is relatively new in the Holy Land. In 1847 Pope Pius IX established the Catholic Patriarchate as a resident see with jurisdiction over the united diocese of Palestine, Transjordan, and Cyprus, the dignity up to that time having been only a titular one. The Roman Catholic Patriarch is the head of the religious community and the representative of the people. Until recently, however, the main authority in Latin affairs in Palestine was vested in the Father Custodian of the Holy Land, at the head of the Franciscan Order, which has been established in Jerusalem since the beginning of the thirteenth century. It is well to note at this point that the Mission of the Franciscans has its origin in the General Chapter, held at the Portiuncula in 1217, when Brother Elias of Cortona was elected Minister of the Province of Syria, and who came to Palestine in 1217 or 1218, followed in 1219 by St. Francis of Assisi himself. Today the Franciscans own considerable valuable property in Palestine and have more convents and institutions there than any other Latin order.

There are many Latin religious orders and institutions in Jerusalem proper, of which the following are probably the most important:

The Franciscan Order with its Convent and Church of St. Saviour. This parish church for the Latins of Jerusalem was rebuilt and consecrated in 1885. The convent contains an orphanage, a parish school for boys, several workshops, an excellent printing establishment, and an important library.

The Hospice of Casa Nova.

The Latin Patriarchate.

The Sisters of St. Joseph of the Apparition, with their French Hospital of St. Louis, established in 1848. The White Fathers, with their Convent and Church of St. Anne, established in 1878. This church is a recently restored crusading abbey, which occupies the site of the home of Joachim and Anna, the parents of the Virgin, according to a fourth century tradition.

The Sisters of the Holy Rosary, arrived in 1880.

The Dominican Fathers, with their Convent and Church of St. Stephen and Biblical and Archaeological School, arrived in 1884.

The Sisters of Charity, arrived in 1886.

The Assumptionist Fathers, with their Hospice of Notre Dame de France, established in 1887.

The Sisters of St. Charles Borromeo, also established in 1887.

The Benedictine Fathers of the Pierre-qui-Vire, arrived in 1889.

The Salesian Fathers and the Salesian Sisters, both arrived in 1904.

The Sisters of Cottolengo, with their Italian Hospital, established in 1919.

The Jesuits, with their Pontifical Biblical Institute, established in 1927.

Other Latin orders and their date of arrival in the Holy Land include: 1873, Carmelite Sisters; 1874, the Fathers of Zion, and the Brothers of the Christian Schools; 1884, Poor Clares; 1885, Franciscan Missionaries of Egypt; 1888, Reparatrice Sisters; 1890, German Lazarists, and the Benedictine Sisters of Calvary; 1903, Passionists; 1904, French Lazarists; 1906, Benedictines of Beuron; 1918, Franciscan Missionaries of Mary; 1919, Sisters of Ivrea; 1922, Sisters of Calvary; 1928, Sisters of St. Dorothea; 1929, Franciscan Tertiary Brothers; 1930, Benedictines of Montserrat; 1931, Polish Sisters of St. Elizabeth; 1933, Franciscan Tertiary Sisters; 1934, Sacred Heart Fathers of Betharram; 1934, the Carmelite Fathers and the Capuchins; and 1935, the Brothers of Consolation of Gethsemane.

In addition to the Roman Catholics in the Holy Land there are small communities representing various Eastern churches, which recognize the supremacy of the Pope, and which may be classed under the term "Uniate Churches." They are as follows: Syrian Jacobites, Melchites, Greek Catholics, Maronites, Armenians, Abyssinians, and Chaldeans. Each is headed either by a Patriarch or by a Bishop in the Holy City. The Holy See is represented in Palestine by an Apostolic Delegate for Egypt, whose jurisdiction extends to Palestine and Transjordan.

THE PROTESTANT DENOMINATIONS

The third and newest of the religious communities represented in Palestine is the Protestant. Protestant denominations did not invade the Holy Land until the year 1840. These groups are very progressive and highly influential; they operate church centers, schools, hospitals and missions.

The body claiming one-third of the Protestant adherents as members is the Anglican Church. At the head of this church is an English bishop, styled the Bishop in Jerusalem and the East. The present occupant of this episcopal throne is the Right Reverend Weston Henry Stewart, raised in Westminster Abbey, September 21, 1943, and his jurisdiction is over Palestine, Syria, Cyprus, and a part of Asia Minor. The bishopric was founded in 1841 by Frederick William IV of Prussia in agreement with England. The primary objects of the new bishopric were the restoration of Christian unity on Catholic principles, and the recovery of episcopal orders through amalgamation with the Greek Orthodox Church. The arrangement provided for an alternate election to the see by England and Prussia, the Archbishop of Canterbury having the right to veto the Prussian vote. The failure to secure episcopal orders for the Lutherans led to the withdrawal of Prussia in 1887, when the joint patronage ceased. The bishopric is especially active today in educational work.

Other major Protestant bodies active in the promotion of Christian ideals among the inhabitants of Palestine include:

The Church of Scotland, with its church and educational institutions in Jerusalem, Jaffa, and Haifa.

The Church Missionary Society, with important schools, orphanages and churches throughout the country.

The London Jews' Society, with its church, school, hospital, and printing establishment in Jerusalem.

The Christian Missionary Alliance.

The Knights of St. John, with its Ophthalmic Hospital in Jerusalem.

The American Society of Friends, which opened schools for girls in 1869 following the visit of Eli and Sibyl Jones. Medical work was maintained for a short period preceding the opening of a boarding school for girls in Ram Allah in 1889. A similar training school was started for boys in 1901. A Monthly Meeting under New England Yearly Meeting was set up in 1890. The Friends also take active interest in the promotion of peace and happiness throughout the land by cooperative, interracial musical endeavors.

The Swedish Jerusalem Society, with its Jerusalem school.

The German Evangelical Society, with its splendid orphanages and workshops.

The German Moravian Mission and their superb Jerusalem Leper Hospital.

The Edinburgh Medical Mission with its outstanding hospitals in Nazareth, Tiberias, and Safad.

The Young Women's Christian Association.

The noteworthy work of the Young Men's Christian Association in Jerusalem.

The Southern Baptist Mission in Jerusalem and Nazareth.

All these Protestant denominational institutions are primarily supported by financial aid secured in the Western world. They are especially important to the future development of Near Eastern music since most Protestant worship services do not demand the use of traditional liturgy. Some groups, but far too few, encourage the use of folk tunes adapted to sacred words, the use of folk hymns, or new hymns composed in the "Eastern idiom" for their meetings for worship. Congregational hymn singing plays an important part in the Near Eastern Protestant church service. Such use helps bring about congregational unity and at the same time provides an opportunity for individual self-expression in worship. Here also lies the rare opportunity, not to be overlooked by the church musician, to preserve the music so close to the hearts of the people, so simple, yet so expressive, so sincere and noble in a humble way.

Various attempts have been made to record the religious folk melodies in remote districts of the Near East for distribution to Protestant centers; but the pioneers were so far apart geographically that conferences for comparisons and plan-making were costly and impractical. Financial aid for such an undertaking has heretofore been impossible to secure, so that persons interested in recording eventually were forced to carry on the work only as a very secondary undertaking, at private expense, and during the so-called rest or vacation periods occasionally granted to missionaries. Naturally little wheat has been gleaned from the vast Near Eastern grainfields of music. Unless harvesters begin organized threshing before too many years pass, the steady and growing influences of Western music will creep over the grainfields like locusts and the bounty will be blemished and lost forever to the world supply of music.

Another gnawing worm in the Near Eastern grain field of

music is the Western missionary who innocently discourages the use of folk music because he finds it "weird." To such a missionary the introduction of Western hymns seems the proper musical background to provide for the native worshiper. Little does he realize that the inclusion of "foreign" melodies in the worship service adds but one more "foreign element" to a service designed to touch and inspire and move individuals tuned to ways-of-living quite different from those of the West.

It is to the Protestant Christian workers that one can look for enlightenment. They alone, of the three great Christian bodies at work in the Holy Land, can preserve and nurture and encourage the use of folk music. The Greek Orthodox Church and the Roman Catholic Church, with their traditional liturgies, do nothing to encourage the use of religious folk music; but at the same time they do little harm to the bountiful store of melody that has sprung from the hearts of the people.

It is with these thoughts that the writer wishes to record in future chapters the fragments of interesting religious folklore, folk custom and tradition, and religious folk music discovered and gathered during free moments while serving in the Holy Land as a missionary under the auspices of the American Friends, during the years 1939–1945.

Although the information is at times very limited and undeveloped, it seems only right that the data gleaned in the Holy Land, just prior to the tragic struggle between Arab and Jew, be organized and recorded, thus preserving the material for future reference and possible expansion, if not completion.

CHAPTER V

The Christmas Pilgrimage

THE Christmas festivity, overshadowed in splendor only by the Eastern Easter celebration, comes to a majestic annual climax on the afternoon and evening of December 24 in the little Palestinian village of Bethlehem. One in search of age-old tradition, folk custom, folk song, and an opportunity to "rub elbows" with Eastern life travels at this season of the year to the village where Christ was born to become part of an imposing pageant, rich in brilliant and clashing color, royal dignity, hushed and anticipated excitement, overwhelming joy, renewed understanding, courage and determination, and contagious gaiety.

Truly the "whole world" meets in Jerusalem at noon on December 24 to join the traditional pilgrimage to the manger where Mary gave birth to the Messiah. The North and the South, the East and West—black, yellow, white, and brown—all in holiday garb fashioned at every corner of the globe, join the august procession of Christians moving toward the Holy City to pay homage to the Christ Child.

Heading the international march of worshipers in the Roman Catholic Christmas procession, the Christmas celebration chosen for detailed description because the date coincides with Western Christmas, are the Roman Catholic Patriarch and hundreds and hundreds of robed priests and nuns representing every Catholic order. Adult choirs and youth choirs, boys' choirs and girls' choirs, bands and scouts and mounted horsemen, all play spectacular roles in the pageant. Down through the Valley of Rephaim, past the Well of the Magi, past Mar Elias, and on through the Field of Peas the procession slowly winds. Flags wave and priceless ban-

25

ners whip madly as the chilly December wind rushes across the valley from the Mediterranean on its journey to the Dead Sea.

As the procession eventually nears Rachel's Tomb, civilian and international diplomatic dignitaries meet the church heads and their followers to join the walk into the village through a narrow isle of closely packed humans. Soldiers, policemen, and scouts are kept busy clearing a path for the religious march. Many weary spectators along the way have stood for hours before the parade to hold a choice spot, hoping all the while that they may be among the fortunate ones to receive a blessing from the Patriarch or that they may be near enough to touch his holy garment.

Onward through the village of Beit Jala the excited march progresses, with but a few lingering long enough to quench their burning thirst at David's Well. Forward into Bethlehem, and at last the steady flow of humanity halts before the narrow doorway leading into the Church of the Nativity.

New pilgrims are truly inspired as they gaze for the first time upon the imposing, yet truly simple, entry into the ancient Church of Churches. Again, they are bewildered to note that every doorway in its magnificent entrance except one that is very narrow and low has been sealed from intruders. Upon inquiry, Bethlehem inhabitants give two folk-reasons for this reconstruction. The first and most probable reason for making the doorway extremely low and narrow, was to keep Turkish horsemen from entering the chapel on horseback—the Turks being in control of the land at the time of these structural changes. The second tradition suggests that respect demands that all who enter the sacred church of Christ's birth should humbly "bow low."

As the Patriarch and his subjects enter the Church patio, the bells of Bethlehem peal out the season's joyous tidings. The priests and nuns and choirs and onlookers join in chanting psalms of praise to the Lord of Love. High Mass is performed for the Christmas pilgrims and followed by reverent visits to the Grotto and on to near-by Shepherds' Field. The celebration continues throughout Christmas Eve and Christmas Day.

The time-honored Christmas Mass begins at ten o'clock Christmas Eve and ends at two o'clock Christmas morning. The main chapel is always crowded with world dignitaries. The robes and costumes of the participating church dignitaries are numerous, magnificent with jewels, gloriously colorful, and costly. At midnight the special Christmas music reaches an exalted climax as the Christ Child, represented by a life-sized doll, is carried to the altar. Later this doll is reverently carried to Rome and sold at auction.

Protestant pilgrims too join the joyous jubilee on December 24 and 25, and for a time all Christianity seems united as of old. Christmas carols so dear to the hearts of all are sung at nine o'clock on Christmas Eve directly below the Bethlehem Bell Tower in the Church of the Nativity compound. These traditional carols, heartily but sincerely sung simultaneously in innumerable tongues, fill the air surrounding the "little village" with songs of praise and thanksgiving in honor and memory of the "Crib of Bethlehem." Immediately following the carol sing, which is internationally broadcast, the Anglicans hold a short service.

Thirteen days after Western Christmas, the Eastern or Greek Orthodox Church commemorates the birth of Christ. Pilgrims will find the celebration similar to the Roman Catholic festivity. However, the Greek Orthodox Patriarch and his procession are met by countless civilian and international diplomatic dignitaries at Mar Elias instead of Rachel's Tomb.

On Christmas Eve, at both Christmas commemorations, camps seem to sprout everywhere, and campfires light the "little town of Bethlehem" for miles around. Truly there is "no place in the inn" for celebrants; but a place for rest is the last thought in the minds of the throng—singing and dancing, drinking and eating the whole night through are the "order of the day," for Christ is born anew in Bethlehem!

WELL OF THE MAGI

. . . and lo, the star which they had seen in the East went before
them . . . When they saw the star, they rejoiced exceedingly with
great joy.[1]

———•◆•———

The distance between the city of Jerusalem and the village of
Bethlehem is approximately ten kilometers, or six miles. At
about kilometer three, one comes into the fertile valley known in
biblical days as the Valley of Rephaim. This plain is known by
the Arabs as El Bukei'a and is generally accepted as being the
Valley of Rephaim, or Valley of Giants. It was the ancient boundary line between the tribes of Judah and Benjamin.[2] The Philistines frequently used it as a camping ground, and here was the
scene of two defeats inflicted on them by David.[3] The pilgrimage
continues on past Beit Safafa and Sherafat, two Arab villages,
then past the traditional tomb of the aged Simeon,[4] with a stop
at approximately kilometer five—halfway between the two holy
cities. At this point, on the left side of the road, is the Well of
the Magi, sometimes called the Well of the Star. Christian tradition, since the sixteenth century, tells us that the three Wise
Men, being weary in their search for the Infant King and having
lost sight of the brilliant star, sat down at this well to rest and
contemplate. Seeking water to quench the thirst of his tired com-
panions and to refresh the faithful camels, one of them leaned
far over the stone well opening to drop his gourd deep into the
water, and again beheld the wondrous star which had guided
them during their long journey from the east, reflected in the
quiet water.

Bir Kadismu ("seat," or "place of rest") is the name given to
this sacred spot by Christian Arabs. The Arabic word is without

---

[1] St. Matthew 2:9–10.
[2] Joshua 15:8.
[3] II Samuel 5:18–22, and 23:12–13.
[4] St. Luke 2:25–35.

doubt a corrupted form of the Greek *kathedra*, "seat." Their charming, age-old legend, possibly founded on a passage in the Proto-Gospel of James, refers to the well as having been the resting place of Mary on her tiresome journey from the distant city of Nazareth to the village of Bethlehem. The legend relates that as Joseph gently helped the Virgin descend from her animal she expressed the wish for a refreshing drink of water. Water sprang suddenly from the near-by rocks to fulfill her desire. Until the seventeenth century, pilgrims saw here, in addition to the well and the rocks, a large terebinth tree which, according to the legend, had lowered and spread its branches to give cool shade for the Holy Family.

About the middle of the fifth century there was on this spot the Ecclesia Kalismathis, a church built by the pious and wealthy matron Icelia in honor of Mary. The celebrated Abbot Theodosius is said to have dwelt near it for some time before beginning his great monastic foundations.

MAR ELIAS

. . . Elijah arose, and went for his life . . . he went a day's journey into the wilderness, and came and sat down under a juniper tree: . . . And as he lay and slept under a juniper tree, behold, then an angel touched him . . .[5]

———•—•———

Ascending the hill from the Well of the Magi, one finds the Greek Orthodox Monastery of Mar Elias on a high plateau commanding a magnificent view of the blue Hills of Moab and the Dead Sea on the east, ancient Herodium to the southeast, the hilltop village of Bethlehem surrounded by its olive trees on the south, and Jerusalem on the north.

The monastery was founded in the sixth century by Bishop Elias, whose tomb was shown in the church as late as the seven-

[5] I Kings 19:1–8.

teenth century. Emperor Manuel Comnenus and the Franks, who found it in ruins after a destructive earthquake, rebuilt it in 1160 under the title of St. Elijah the Prophet.

The tradition connecting this site with the flight of Elijah from the vengeance of Jezebel originated about the time of the Crusaders. The elongated depression in the rock opposite the monastery gate marks the spot where the prophet is said to have rested, making the depression with the weight of his body.

FRANK MOUNTAIN, THE ANCIENT HERODIUM

Jebel Fureidis (that is, in Arabic, Hill of Paradise), or Frank Mountain, the ancient Herodium, is first viewed from the high plateau upon which the Greek Orthodox Monastery of Mar Elias is erected. It is a half-day's journey by foot from Bethlehem. The partly artificial conical summit of this mount still shows traces of the fortress and palace built by Herod the Great. It is here that Herod was buried, shortly after the massacre at Bethlehem of innocent children by his command. Archaeologists have found no trace of his sepulcher, however.

Near Frank Mountain is the labyrinthine grotto which tradition has identified with the Cave of Adullam, the scene of David's and Saul's meeting.[6] South of this is the village of Teku'—the ancient Tekoa, home of the prophet Amos.[7]

THE FIELD OF THE GRAY PEAS

Just beyond Mar Elias, on the left side of the road, is a field covered with innumerable little gray pebbles. The legend is told that Christ once passed this field and lovingly called to a sower: "Greetings, my friend, and what are you so busily sowing today?" "Stones," replied the disgruntled farmer without so much as turning to see the passing traveler or to exchange the

---

[6] I Samuel 22:1, II Samuel 23:13, and I Chronicles 11:15.
[7] II Chronicles 11:6 and Amos 1:1.

customary greetings. Some months later when the peasant and his family returned to the field to gather in the peas at harvest time, they found, to their utter amazement, nothing but petrified peas. "Truly," the remorseful farmer whispered, "I planted stones."

Today many of these stones are seen scattered upon the flat rock where visiting pilgrims collect the pebbles as reminders of the punishment that follows a lie.

RACHEL'S TOMB

And Rachel died, and was buried in the way to Ephrath, which is Bethlehem. And Jacob set a pillar upon her grave: that is the pillar of Rachel's grave unto this day.[8]

———•—•———

At about kilometer seven on the road from Jerusalem to Bethlehem is Rachel's Tomb, known to the Arabs as Kubbet Rahil. It has been an object of veneration during forty centuries for the Jews, the Christians, and the Moslems. The Jews are the custodians of the sacred tomb, and it is worthy of note that this is almost the only instance of Jewish ownership of a holy site.

The tomb consists of an oblong building with an arched entrance on the north. It is divided into two rooms, the eastern room being a vestibule for Muhammedan worship. It contains a prayer niche, or mihrab, indicating the direction of Mecca. The western chamber contains a large masonry cenotaph thought to cover the place of interment of the beloved wife of Jacob, and in this room the Jews perform their devotions. It is surmounted by a whitewashed dome, typical of Palestinian *wilis*.

Tradition has long identified this spot as the sepulcher of Rachel, and throughout the early Christian period it was marked by a mound of stones. The monument underwent some altera-

[8] Genesis 35:19–20. For a contradictory biblical passage referring to the burial place of Rachel see I Samuel 10:2.

tions during the fifteenth century and has been repeatedly restored since.

BEIT JALA

The Christian village of Beit Jala has been identified by archaeologists with three different ancient places: Gallim; [9] Giloh, the home of Ahithophel; [10] and Zelzah.[11] The flourishing little village of about three thousand inhabitants is chiefly made up of Greek Orthodox Christians. It is on the slope of a hill covered with vineyards, is noted for its excellent apricots, and is in the midst of the largest olive orchards in Palestine.

DAVID'S WELL

And David longed, and said, Oh that one would give me drink of the water of the well of Bethlehem, which is by the gate! [12]

Climbing the hill to Bethlehem proper, one passes an enclosure with an iron gate. This contains the so-called David's Well. Tradition dating back to the fifteenth century identifies it as "the well of Bethlehem which is by the gate." From this well three mighty men brought David water at the risk of their lives, passing through the hostile "host of the Philistines," who were garrisoned in Bethlehem and encamped on the Plain of Rephaim.

Near the well is a beautiful mosaic floor bearing a Greek inscription from the Psalms. Some archaeologists have suggested that the floor may be a remnant from the huge hospice for pilgrims or from a monastery founded by St. Paula during the late fourth century.

A necropolis near by has not received archaeological identification.

9 Isaiah 10:30 and I Samuel 25:44.
10 II Samuel 15:12 and Joshua 15:51.
11 I Samuel 10:2.
12 II Samuel 23:14–17 and 1 Chronicles 11:17–18.

BETHLEHEM OF JUDEA

. . . Ephrath; the same is Bethlehem.[13]

But thou, Bethlehem Ephratah, though thou be little among the thousands of Judah, yet out of thee shall he come forth unto me that is to be ruler in Israel; whose goings forth have been from of old, from everlasting.[14]

———◆◆———

The village of Bethlehem, one of the oldest hamlets of Palestine and second only to Jerusalem in historical interest, is the scene of many important events in biblical history. Near here Rachel died; this was the home of Naomi; [15] here was consummated the beautiful idyll of Ruth the Moabitess and Boaz, the progenitors of David and of Christ.[16] Bethlehem was the native place of Jesse and David,[17] and here the Prophet anointed David, King over Israel.[18] Later we hear of a Philistine garrison in Beth-

13 Genesis 48:7.
14 Micah 5:2.
15 Ruth 1:19–21.
16 Ruth 4:9–13.
17 Ruth 4:22.
18 I Samuel 16:1, 13.

lehem,[19] fortified with walls and towers. It was made strategically stronger by Rehoboam.[20]

In gratitude for the services that Barzillai the Gileadite had rendered during the revolt of Absalom, when he was beyond the Jordan, David brought the aged Barzillai's son Chimham to Jerusalem and undoubtedly showered benefits upon him and probably gave him part of the land of his own native town.[21] To shelter his numerous flocks and herds and to serve as a station for caravans on their way to Egypt, Chimham erected near Bethlehem an immense caravanserai. The Prophet Jeremiah relates that the Jews, having decided to fly for safety to the banks of the Nile after the murder of Gedaliah,[22] "dwelt in the habitation [Khan Chimham] of Chimham, which is by Bethlehem." [23] It is probable that six hundred years later Mary and Joseph presented themselves at this same Khan, seeking lodging for the night.

As the birthplace of the child Jesus, Bethlehem has gained immortality—it will reign forever a city of cities.[24] Within its walls and towers, soon after his birth, occurred the terrible massacre of infants by the bloodthirsty and cruel Herod.[25] During the time of Justin Martyr, in the second century, there is an unauthenticated story to the effect that Emperor Hadrian profaned the town by bringing in the worship of false gods; namely, that of Adonis. But St. Helena and Emperor Constantine, in A.D. 330, made it one of the most glorious sanctuaries of Christendom by erecting the magnificent Basilica. From that time forth Bethlehem became one of the great monastic centers. There St. Jerome took up his abode in 384, in one of the grottoes near the spot sanctified by the birth of Christ, and lived until his death in 420 at the

19 II Samuel 23:14.
20 II Chronicles 11:5–6.
21 II Samuel 19:31–40 and I Kings 2:7.
22 Jeremiah 41:2.
23 Jeremiah 41:17.
24 St. Luke 2:16.
25 St. Matthew 2:16.

age of ninety-two. St. Jerome, born a pagan, was a student of the classic writers, but was commanded in a vision, according to tradition, to renounce this study. He then learned Hebrew and made the Vulgate translation of the Old Testament. St. Paula and her daughter, St. Eustochium, followed St. Jerome to Bethlehem in 386 and founded a nunnery over which Paula presided as abbess, a monastery for St. Jerome and his friends, and a huge hospice for pilgrims who flocked to the village. Paula and Eustochium were Roman ladies of great learning and piety. They were converts to Christianity and studied the Bible under St. Jerome before following him to Bethlehem. Paula was buried in the rock tomb beneath the church, beside her friend and master.

Because Bethlehem was poorly protected, it was sacked by the rebels during the Samaritan revolt of 521–530. In 531, however, Justinian restored its walls, and by 600 it was again a flourishing town with many churches and monasteries. The Persians spared it in 614, and the Arabians in 638. This prosperity ceased for a time when, in 1099, the Arabs destroyed the place as the Crusading host advanced; but the Franks were not slow to rebuild it and to provide it with a castle. It was devastated by the Khwarazmians in 1244, and the walls were demolished in 1263. The Franciscans established themselves near the sanctuary in the thirteenth century, and in 1489 the city was again in ruins. John Zullard writes during this century that nothing was left except

perhaps a few little houses inhabited by certain poor Moors, who live on that little which they earn working and murdering the pilgrims; among whom there are also some Christian Syrians, who nearly all speak a little Italian which they call Frank.

Stagnation and decline followed, but during the last three centuries Bethlehem has recovered. In the early nineteenth century the Bedouins encroached upon it on the edge of the desert, from time to time, and there was conflict and bloodshed between Christians and Moslems. In 1831, however, the Christians expelled the Moslems, and three years later Ibrahim Pasha ordered the destruction of the Muhammedan quarter. From that time onward the little town prospered with a population almost entirely Christian. The Greek Orthodox Church, the Roman Catholic Church, and some Protestant denominations today maintain churches, educational institutions, or medical centers in or near it, and the Moslems maintain one small mosque.

The Bible calls the village Bethlehem of Judea, to distinguish it from the Bethlehem of the tribe of Zebulun in Galilee. The prosperous town of our day is 2,550 feet above sea level, on two ridges forming a semicircle around and above the Valley of the Carob Tree (Wady el Kharroubeh) to the north and bounded on the south by the Valley of the Priest (Wady el Rahib). It is divided into eight districts with an estimated population of 10,000, all Christian except about 300 Moslems. Its inhabitants, who are thought to be descended from the Crusaders with an admixture of Syrian and Arabian blood, are distinguished among the surrounding peoples for their energy and intelligence. The Bethlehem women, with their fine bearing and old-world costume, quaint and picturesque, are noted for their beauty. There are some 2,000 dwellings built of the native reddish stone. The hills are terraced in a succession of vines, olives, almonds, and figs down to the valleys which stretch out on every side except the northwest. In the spring the valleys to the east and south are green.

THE CHURCH OF THE NATIVITY

The old, old story tells us that Joseph and Mary traveled from Nazareth to Bethlehem to be enrolled according to the decree of Caesar Augustus,[26] and that upon their arrival in the city of

[26] St. Luke 2:1.

David there was no room for them in the inn.[27] Therefore, writes
St. Justin the Martyr,

having failed to find any lodging in the town, Joseph sought shelter
in a neighbouring cavern of Bethlehem where Mary "brought forth
her first-born son and laid him in a manger."

Justin the Martyr, a Christian apologist of the second century,
was born in Flavia Neapolis, a Roman city of Samaria. He was
converted about 135 to Christianity and lived in Rome for some
time. It is said that he was beheaded in the reign of Marcus Aure-
lius because he refused to offer sacrifice to the heathen gods. His
works are important as a source of knowledge about Christianity
in the second century.

Undoubtedly the cavern referred to by St. Justin was one of
the caves so frequent in Palestine, used as shelters for animals
in the cold winter nights, where the traditional ox and ass might
well have leaned down over the Christ Child. It was probably
the lower part of Khan Chimham, the inn in which the Holy
Family had earlier sought shelter in vain. At least one is certain
that as early as the second century tradition identified a cave near
Bethlehem with the scene of Christ's birth. Undoubtedly this
grotto early became the object of veneration; according to St.
Jerome, Emperor Hadrian, who made every effort to erase every
vestige of Christian worship from Palestine,

endeavoured also to wipe out the remembrance of Christ's birth by
defiling the grotto by the worship of false gods. Our Bethlehem, the
most august spot in the universe, was overshadowed by a wood consecrated to Thamuz (Adonis), and in the grotto which had heard the
tender wailings of the infant Christ, men bemoaned the "beloved
Venus."

Apparently this effort to defile the grotto did not last long, for
Origen could write at the beginning of the third century:

[27] St. Luke 2:7.

[If] anyone desires to satisfy himself that Jesus was born in Bethlehem, let him know that, in accordance with the Gospel narrative, at Bethlehem is shown the grotto where he first saw the light. Everybody knows it, and the pagans themselves will tell again and again, that in the said cavern was born a certain Jesus, whom the Christians admire and adore.

In the first half of the fourth century, St. Helena "transformed the cave into a splendid sanctuary," and, as has already been noted, Constantine in 330 adorned the sanctuary in a regal style, eclipsing even the magnificence of his mother's design. Findings in 1934 revealed, beneath the pavement of the present Basilica, the true magnificence of the Constantine construction. The primitive pavement is thirty-two inches lower than the present floor and is covered with majestic mosaics.

The work done under St. Jerome, St. Paula, and St. Eustochium in the later fourth century and the early fifth has been mentioned. The Basilica suffered considerable damage in 529 during the Samaritan revolt but was restored in 531 by Emperor Justinian, his architect making considerable alterations in the original design.

When the Persians captured the city in 614 they recognized their national costume in that worn by the Three Kings, representing the Adoration of the Magi in mosaic on the façade of the building, and so did not dare to touch the glorious monument. In 638 the honorable caliph Omar worshiped in the southern apse of the church; but, in order that this sacred site might remain in the possession of the Christians, he forbade his coreligionists to go there to pray except in small numbers. This order was not infringed upon until the ninth and tenth centuries.

Of all the caliphs, al-Hakim alone attempted to lay sacrilegious hands on this sanctuary, in 1010. In his general destruction of churches the Church of the Nativity, it is claimed, miraculously escaped. The Crusaders were surprised to find it uninjured. *

On June 7, 1099, the inhabitants of Bethlehem invited Godfrey de Bouillon, then encamped at Emmaus, to take possession of the town and protect the church. Tancred left Emmaus at the dead of night with one hundred picked knights, and at the break of day his banner was floating over the Basilica. Godfrey de Bouillon, one of the leaders of the First Crusade and the first Latin ruler of Jerusalem, was elected "Baron and Defender of the Holy Sepulcher." He held this dignity about a year and died July 17 or 18, 1100. On Christmas Day, 1101, Baldwin I, brother of the first crusader King of Jerusalem, was crowned in the revered Bethlehem sanctuary. In 1110 Bethlehem was raised to the rank of an episcopal see. It is important to note here that all accounts of medieval pilgrims present a striking uniformity with regard to the church, making it highly improbable that it could have been altered.

In the twelfth century, however, it was thoroughly restored, and the Byzantine Emperor Manuel Comnenus (1143–1180) caused the walls to be richly beautified with gilded mosaics and paintings in the best Byzantine style. The restoration, achieved in common by Greek and Roman Catholics, had the support of Amalric I, King of Jerusalem. This evidence of friendship, which at the time seemed a prelude to the reunion of the two churches, terminated in 1169.

Saladin, the Sultan, conquered Bethlehem in 1178 but respected the church. He was described by his biographers as chivalrous, just, generous, and high-minded; most tender-hearted, pious in his life, never indulging in anything reprehensible or unseemly, and devoted to his people's welfare. Tradition states that Saladin not only respected the Church of the Nativity in Bethlehem but, on approaching the city of Jerusalem, sent for the principal inhabitants and spoke to them in the following terms: "I know, as you do, that Jerusalem is a holy place. I do not wish to profane it by the effusion of blood; abandon your ramparts, and I shall give to you a part of my treasures and as much land as you can cultivate." With characteristic fanaticism the Crusaders refused this generous and humane offer. Irritated by their refusal, Saladin vowed he would avenge on the city the butchery committed by the comrades and soldiers of Godfrey de Bouillon. After the siege had lasted awhile the Crusaders lost heart, and appealed for mercy "in the name of the common Father of mankind." The Sultan's kindness of heart conquered his desire for punishment. The Greek and Syrian Christians within Jerusalem received permission to abide in the Sultan's dominions in the full enjoyment of their civil rights, and the Franks and Latins who wished to settle in Palestine as subjects of the Sultan were permitted to do so.

The clergy and the people carried away all their treasures and valuables without the smallest molestation. Several Christians were seen carrying on their shoulders their feeble and aged parents or friends. Touched by the spectacle, the Sultan distributed a goodly sum to them in charity, and even provided them with mules. He restored to mothers their sons, to wives their husbands. He distributed liberal alms among the orphans and widows, and allowed the Knights Hospitalers, although they had been in arms against him, to continue their work of tending the sick and wounded and looking after the Christian pilgrims.

On Friday, the 27th of Rajab (the anniversary of the Vision of the Ascension of the Prophet), A.D. 583, attended by the princes and lords and the dignitaries of the empire who had arrived in camp to congratulate him on his victory, Saladin entered Jerusalem.

Hubert Walter, Bishop of Salisbury, taking advantage of the truce concluded between the King of England and Saladin, secured once again in 1192 the right to perform the Roman Catholic liturgy in the Basilica, under the clause that the faithful should pay tribute. It was agreed that two priests with their deacons, and a small body of indigenous Catholic clergy, should be attached to each of the sanctuaries of Bethlehem, Jerusalem, and Nazareth. It would be well to note here that after the fall of the Roman Empire in 1187, the Canons Regular of St. Augustine, who had served the Basilica, were succeeded by the Franciscans.

Records testify to their possession of the Grotto and their use and upkeep of the Basilica during the fourteenth and fifteenth centuries. At the end of the fourteenth century, Gerardo Calveti, Guardian of Mount Zion, traveled all over Europe to induce the Christian princes to help in the restoration of the holy site.

In 1482 Edward IV of England and Philip, Duke of Burgundy, joined in supplying materials for the repair of the dilapidated roof of the venerable building, Philip supplying the pine wood from Venice and Edward the sheets of lead to cover the new tim-berwork. The Republic of Venice undertook the transport of the materials to Jaffa, and the Franciscans directed the work. It is interesting to record here that in the early part of the seventeenth century the Turks, thinking they could put the leaden strips of the church roof to a better use, took them down and made bullets of them.

During the twenty-four-year war between the Ottoman Empire and the Republic of Venice which ended in 1669 with the expulsion of the Venetians from Crete, the Greeks were authorized to renew the roofing of the Basilica and take over the Grotto.

The Roman Catholics retook the Grotto in 1690 and held it until 1757, when the Greeks took possession once more of the Basilica and, inside the crypt, the Altar of the Nativity. The Catholics did not again obtain a share in the proprietorship of the church until 1852.

In 1717 the Roman Catholics placed a new silver star in the Grotto to replace the older one, which had worn out; and they claim ownership of the Altar of the Nativity because of this. The star, said to mark the spot of the immaculate birth, was regarded with extreme jealousy by the rival sects and was torn off or stolen more than once, and it finally disappeared on October 12, 1847. After five years of negotiating and the intervention of Napoleon III, Sultan Abdul Mejid presented the church with a star similar to the one which had disappeared, which gave neither of the rivals the possession. This was sealed into place in 1853.

In the early years of the twentieth century some of the nails holding the star in position disappeared and naturally had to be replaced. None of the rival sects would permit another to make the replacement, and it was not until the Turkish authorities brought in a Muhammedan gypsy-smith to make the repairs that the heated quarrels subsided. Police are always on guard in this chapel to prevent the encroachment or aggression of any faction. Thus peace is maintained at the point of a sword on the spot of the birth of the Prince of Peace.

Records show very few and minor alterations or restorations of the church in the past one hundred years. Today this venerable pile of stone gives the aspect of a fortress. The sacred structure is made up of a vast congeries of churches and monasteries clustered around the original or central church. This remains practically unaltered since it was built by Constantine and, with the main apse, belongs to the Greek Orthodox Church. In 1842 the Greeks erected a wall which completely divided the nave from the transept; but the wall was taken down in 1918, and the symmetry of the Church restored.

Under the central part of the transept is the Grotto, or Chapel, of the Nativity. Two flights of steps, from the two sides of the great choir, descend to the Grotto and meet before the Altar of the Nativity. The Grotto is forty feet long from east to west, twelve feet wide, and ten feet high. It is lighted by thirty-two lamps. The walls are lined with marble, and the floor is paved with the same material. Pilgrims chipped so many pieces of rock off the wall for relics and souvenirs that it became necessary to cover the side walls with amianthus, guaranteed against fire, and this belongs to the Franciscans. This covering was a present given in 1874 by President MacMahon of France.

The Grotto contains the Altar of the Nativity, the Chapel of the Manger, and the Altar of the Adoration of the Magi. In the floor under the altar in the small east apse is a silver star with the simple Latin inscription, "Hic de Virgine Maria Jesus Christus Natus Est." Over the star burn fifteen lamps, of which six belong to the Greeks, five to the Armenians, and four to the Roman

Catholics. This spot was highly decorated as far back as the time of Constantine, and a few ancient mosaics are still visible. The altar has also been venerated by the Moslems.

The Chapel of the Manger is opposite the Altar of the Nativity and down three steps. By tradition, this is the site of the manger in which Mary laid her child. The spot is marked now by a marble manger on the east side, containing the wax effigy of an infant over which are hung lamps. One object of beauty has been placed here, a painting of the Nativity by Schmalz. The present manger was installed sometime after the removal of the original in the eighth century to Rome, where it can be seen in the Church of Santa Maria Maggiore.

Near the Manger is an altar dedicated to the Wise Men. It was built, tradition claims, over the site where the three Wise Men "saw the child with Mary his mother, and fell down and worshiped him. Then, opening their treasures, they offered him gifts, gold and frankincense and myrrh."

The existing buildings include the Armenian Monastery, an old buttressed building; the Church of St. Catherine; the Chapel of the Innocents; the Chapel of St. Joseph; the Tomb and Altar of St. Eusebius of Cremona; the Chapel of St. Jerome; the massively built Franciscan Monastery with its Garden of St. Jerome; the Greek Orthodox Church of St. George; and the Greek Orthodox Monastery, which adjoins the Basilica on the south and possesses the tower containing the world-famous Christmas Bells.

The Roman Catholic Church of St. Catherine marks the traditional site of Christ's appearance to St. Catherine of Alexandria and prediction of her martyrdom. In the fourteenth century a Chapel of St. Nicholas is mentioned, which was in all probability the predecessor of this church. The present building was erected by the Franciscans in 1881.

The Chapel of the Innocents is below the Church of St. Catherine and is actually a rock-hewn continuation of the Grotto. A tradition of the fifteenth century identifies it as the scene of the murder by Herod of some Bethlehem infants who had been concealed for safety here by their mothers. These children are revered as the first to have shed their blood for Christ.

A flight of five steps leads from the Chapel of the Innocents to a room where, it is said, Joseph received the warning from the angel to flee into Egypt. This sanctuary is known as the Chapel of St. Joseph.

Records disclose that the presbyter Eusebius of Cremona was a pupil of St. Jerome. There is no record, however, of his having died and been buried in Bethlehem. Be that as it may, the Roman Catholics declare him St. Jerome's successor as superior of the monastery, and his tomb and altar can be viewed by pilgrims there today. The first known record connecting Eusebius with the existing grotto, officially titled the Tomb and Altar of St. Eusebius of Cremona, is in the sixteenth century. He should not be confused with the Eusebius who was Bishop of Cremona in the seventh century.

The Tomb of St. Jerome has been shown in connection with holy sites in the greater church compound for three centuries. The tombs of his pupils, St. Paula and her daughter St. Eustochium, on the opposite side of the chapel, have been shown since the sixteenth century. They were, however, formerly to the south of the church.

The Chapel of St. Jerome is thought to be on the site of the cell in which he made his famous Vulgate translation of the Bible in Latin and wrote his voluminous commentaries on the Holy Scriptures. Although lined with masonry, it is cut out of the rock. The present chapel, which was first shown in 1445, formerly also contained the saint's tomb. An aged painting of St. Jerome holding a Bible is on display.

The Protestants do not maintain a separate chapel in connection with the Church of the Nativity, but, as the Greek Orthodox Church adheres to the old calendar and their Christmas therefore comes later in the year, the Church of England holds a special midnight service in the little Greek Church of St. George. The annual midnight liturgies performed on Christmas Eve attract hundreds of pilgrims, and the jubilant midnight ringing of the Bells of Bethlehem and the joyous and lusty singing of traditional carols announcing the rebirth of the Prince of Peace are broadcast the world around.

Indeed, the Church of the Nativity is the scene of colorful annual celebrations, and the birthplace of the Christ Child is the scene of perpetual adoration.

SHEPHERDS' FIELD

And in that region there were shepherds out in the field, keeping watch over their flock by night. And an angel of the Lord appeared to them, and the glory of the Lord shone around them, and they were filled with fear. And the angel said to them, "Be not afraid; for behold, I bring you good news of a great joy which will come to all the people; for to you is born this day in the city of David a Savior, who is Christ the Lord. And this will be a sign for you: you will find a babe wrapped in swaddling cloths and lying in a manger." And suddenly there was with the angel a multitude of the heavenly host praising God and saying, "Glory to God in the highest, and on earth peace among men with whom he is pleased!"

When the angels went away from them into heaven, the shepherds said to one another, "Let us go over to Bethlehem and see this thing that has happened, which the Lord has made known to us." And they went with haste, and found Mary and Joseph, and the babe lying in a manger.[28]

———•———

The Christmas pilgrimage to the little town of Bethlehem and the Church of the Nativity is filled with Eastern color and gaiety, tradition and ceremony. The joyous celebration is unequaled in the West. However, a second pilgrimage on Christmas evening is outstanding to the Protestant pilgrim for the conspicuous absence of screaming color, splendor, and ritual.

[28] St. Luke 2:8–16.

The walk to near-by Shepherds' Field is hushed and profoundly peaceful. One leaves the laughter and the singing, the dancing and feasting—color and lights and boisterous rejoicing—in Bethlehem to descend a stony path eastward from the Church of the Nativity, past the Milk Grotto, pausing on the hilltop only long enough to marvel at the breath-taking view of the village of Beit Sahur en Nasara and its surrounding vineyards dotted with picturesque watchtowers. On into the calm of the night, past the chapel built in honor of St. Joseph, to the "cistern" in the heart of the village of Beit Sahur, which is said to have afforded the Virgin a drink, its waters miraculously rising to the surface, after the inhospitable inhabitants had refused to draw water for her.

In peaceful Meditation one continues past the Greek Orthodox Monastery, called Deir er Rum in Arabic. Just before reaching the field, identified by tradition as Shepherds' Field, one crosses the small fertile plain known as the Field of Boaz. Here, according to tradition, the beautiful Moabitess gleaned the ears of corn (wheat) that the reapers had purposely overlooked. Here also Ruth met her future husband, the generous Boaz.

Then at last to a refreshing and rewarding pause in Shepherds' Field. Here one can lie flat or lean contentedly on the trunk of a rugged olive tree and gaze at the distant lights of Bethlehem, hear the far-away carolers and the ringing of the Christmas bells. Especially here and on the shores of the Sea of Galilee, one can find heavenly stillness and the opportunity to wait and meditate and find a new source of strength and understanding and courage and conviction.

Shepherds' Field, surrounded with its Grotto of the Shepherds by a high stone wall, is on the traditional site where shepherds kept "watch over their flock by night" and the angel appeared before them to announce to them the birth of the Messiah in near-by Bethlehem. It was here that "a multitude of the heavenly host" broke forth in strains of heavenly music. This terraced area is covered with rocks, contains many olive trees and grapevines, and ruins of ancient churches are scattered over it. The Grotto is a Greek Orthodox chapel, converted from what was undoubtedly a cistern at one time. Twenty-one steps descend into the subterranean chapel, which contains paintings, remains of a medieval mosaic floor, and some shafts of columns. The Grotto of the Shepherds is not kept open to pilgrims; but the key is to be had at the Greek monastery in near-by Beit Sahur upon payment of a gratuity. The Arabic name is Deir er Ra'wat, Convent of the Flocks.

In the fifth century, some say before the year 385, there arose on this spot a sanctuary in honor of the shepherds. It was called Poimenion, "of the flock" or "of the sheepfold." In the days of Paula, the pupil of St. Jerome, the Tower of Edar, or Tower of Flocks,[29] was shown in the Shepherds' Field. In the time of Arculfus (seventh century) a fine church containing the bones of the shepherds occupied the site. The ruins about the grotto are thought by some to be the remains of these earlier sanctuaries or of the Crusader Church of Gloria in Excelsis. Others identify this Frankish building with the ruins, on the knoll about seven hundred yards to the north, of a church that had three aisles and a square tower. These later ruins are called Siar al-Ghanem, the Sheepfold, by native Christians.

A second journey from Bethlehem to Shepherds' Field calls for more leisure so that all the holy and traditional biblical sites can be visited. The first one of interest is the Milk Grotto, or Women's Cavern, a cave of irregular shape hollowed out of soft white rock. In the court stands a beautiful statue of the Virgin. The grotto derives its name from the legend that the Holy Family at one time took shelter in it. While Mary was suckling the overzealous Christ Child a few drops of her milk fell to the stone floor and turned it suddenly a chalky white. This grotto is a favorite place of pilgrimage for both Christian and Moslem women who lack sufficient milk while nursing their offspring.

[29] Genesis 35:21 and Micah 4:8.

The superstitious women go to it to pray, then break off a piece of the soft rock and return home to grind this to powder. The powder is mixed with their food or drink, and is supposed to rejuvenate their supply of milk in time. Little round cakes are now made, mixed with the powdered stone, and sold to visiting pilgrims. The superstition goes so far as to claim the dust will increase the milk even of animals.

The next pause of prime importance is at the House of St. Joseph, a chapel upon the site of an earlier church dedicated to St. Joseph, which in turn, according to medieval tradition, was built where the Holy Family had lived until their flight into Egypt. Here, tradition tells us, "an angel of the Lord appeared to Joseph in a dream and said, 'Rise, take the child and his mother, and flee to Egypt, and remain there till I tell you; for Herod is about to search for the child, to destroy him.' " [30]

Most pilgrims make a last significant stop, before continuing through the Field of Boaz to the final destination in Shepherds' Field, to roam the paths of Beit Sahur en Nasara, which the native Christians prefer to call Village of the Shepherds. It has approximately 1,800 inhabitants, most of whom are members of the Greek Orthodox community. Although ancient flint instruments have been found in the caves of the village, the first known mention of Beit Sahur is by pilgrims in the sixteenth century. It has been identified, however, with Ashur in connection with Tekoa.[31] Beit Sahur is now said to have been the dwelling place of the shepherds.

[30] St. Matthew 2:13.
[31] I Chronicles 2:24.

TODAY CHRIST IS BORN

1

Today came He
Who from Mary was born.
Mercy He gave to sinners
By His redeeming blood.

2

O Come and glorify His name!
Lift your voice in song
Because He opened the way
To the glory of a new life.

3

He gave unto us through His death
Everlasting and eternal life.
Let us follow Him
The giver of riches and blessings.

SAVE US, O SON OF MAN

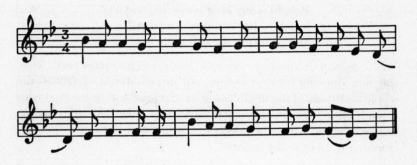

Christmas

1

Save us, O Son of man!
Thou, of a virgin born!
Let us praise Thee
Hallelu, Hallelu!

2

Save us, O Son of man!
On this Christmas morn
We praise Thee
Hallelu, Hallelu!

CHAPTER VI

The Palm Sunday Pilgrimage

> Tell the daughter of Zion,
> Behold, your king is coming to you,
> humble, and mounted on an ass,
> and on a colt, the foal of an ass.[1]

. . . as he rode along, they spread their garments on the road. As he was now drawing near, at the descent of the Mount of Olives, the whole multitude of the disciples began to rejoice and praise God with a loud voice for all the mighty works that they had seen, saying, "Blessed be the King who comes in the name of the Lord! Peace in heaven and glory in the highest!" [2]

"Hosanna! Blessed be he who comes in the name of the Lord! Blessed be the kingdom of our father David that is coming! Hosanna in the highest!" [3]

———•———

PALM SUNDAY in the Holy City of Jerusalem is indeed the re-enactment of a portion of the Scriptures. Christians from far and near travel early to the Golden City to climb the Mount of Olives and cross over into Bethphage to join the Palm Sunday parade. Hundreds and hundreds of Roman Catholic priests and nuns, school and church choirs, and numerous pilgrims form a triumphant procession into the Holy City waving freshly hewn palm branches, spreading fronds and foliage, and strewing the path with spring flowers. At the head of the parade rides the Roman Catholic Patriarch, upon a young colt.

[1] St. Matthew 21:5.
[2] St. Luke 19:36–38.
[3] St. Mark 11:9–10.

Truly the joyous and exultant singing is uplifting. Truly Christ again is crowned, Hosanna in the highest! Leaving ancient Bethphage behind, the parade winds through the narrow lanes on the Mount of Olives, past the Chapel of the Ascension and the Church of the Lord's Prayer. Gaily through the Garden of Gethsemane, the procession sweeps, on past the Basilica of Gethsemane and the Basilica of the Agony—forgetting all the while the sufferings of Christ, remembering only His majestic victories; on with delightful songs and vigorous palm waving the jubilant crowd surges, past the Church of the Virgin and the Church of St. Anne, until the destination is finally reached. At the Twin Pools of Bethesda the Patriarch dismounts, and the pilgrims join in the celebration of High Mass. Following the service, the celebrants start their homeward journey, palm branch in hand, eager to arrive and adorn the entry into their home with all cherished branches so proudly borne by members of the family in the triumphant procession. At the end of the long day, all are weary but happy to have been actors in a great Christian drama.

BETHPHAGE

When he drew near to Bethphage and Bethany, at the mount that is called Olivet, he sent two of the disciples, saying, "Go into the village opposite, where on entering you will find a colt tied, on which no one has ever yet sat; untie it and bring it here. If any one asks you, 'Why are you untying it?' you shall say this, 'The Lord has need of it.' " [4]

———— • • ————

The Sanctuary of Bethphage is built upon the remains of a twelfth century Crusader church on the traditional site of Bethphage. In this village Christ secured and mounted the colt of an ass upon which he made his triumphal entry into Jerusalem. Inside the chapel is a cubical block of stone which tradition calls the identical one upon which Jesus set foot while mounting the

[4] St. Luke 19:29–31. Also read St. Matthew 21:1–3 and St. Mark 11:1–4.

colt. The stone was accidentally uncovered in the rocky soil in 1876. Its four sides are covered with fragments of delicate paintings, "more like illuminations in a costly Missal than frescoes intended to cover the bareness of a stone." The painting on the north side represents a fortress or a castle, a group of men, an ass, and her colt. The east side represents a procession of people bearing palms. On the south side, facing the village of Bethany, two women undoubtedly represent Mary and Martha, prostrate at the feet of Jesus. The background scene probably represents the resurrection of their brother, Lazarus. On the west side a mutilated inscription in four lines carries the name Bethphage, and the place which should represent Jesus mounting the ass is effaced.

Tradition also asserts that it was here that "Martha heard that Jesus was coming," and "went and met him, while Mary sat in the house." Martha, the sister of Lazarus of Bethany, then said to Jesus, "Lord, if you had been here, my brother would not have died." Shortly Mary "came where Jesus was" and "fell at his feet, saying to him, 'Lord, if you had been here, my brother would not have died.' " [5]

CHAPEL OF THE ASCENSION

Then he led them out as far as Bethany, and lifting up his hands he blessed them. While he blessed them, he parted from them. And they returned to Jerusalem with great joy.[6]

———————

In the midst of the Arab village of Kafr et Tur, on the southern summit of the Mount of Olives, is the Chapel of the Ascension. The acceptance by Occidentals of this spot as that of the Ascension is very ancient, in spite of the fact that St. Luke says explicitly that "he led them out as far as Bethany" at the time of

[5] St. John 11:1–37.
[6] St. Luke 24:50–52.

His Ascension. In view of this convincing evidence, the Crusaders were still firmly convinced of the claims of this spot as the authentic one and not one placed in the village of Bethany.

In A.D. 351 Constantine the Great erected a small, roofless chapel on the site. The archaeological analysis of the remains allows one to recognize the ancient building in the octagonal form to which the present chapel adheres. The original was enclosed by a circular wall, with an internal row of concentric columns supporting a circular drum surmounted by a cupola pierced with a great opening in the center. The present building contains only a few stones of the original outer wall, some being located at the base columns and others in the central arcaded edifice. The existing cupola contains some of the material used by the Moslems in their 1200 construction.

In the seventh century the monk Modestus built a church here, which was destroyed in the eleventh. In 1187 the chapel was transformed into a mosque. The present chapel, dating from 1835, is still the property of the Moslems; but Christians are permitted to hold mass in it on certain days. This chapel, or mosque, adjoins an interesting dervish monastery which was originally an Augustinian abbey. Inside the chapel, in an enclosed oblong piece of marble, is shown the sacred rock in which legend sees the impression of the right foot of Jesus, left by him when ascending into heaven. This "footprint" is obviously just a modern mark to preserve the site.

In the chapel courtyard are Armenian, Coptic, Syrian, and Greek altars. Inside the monastery, in the southwest corner, is a door to the grotto of St. Pelagia—Rahibet Bint Hassan in Arabic. Pelagia was an actress of Antioch who, according to Crusader tradition, came here in the fifth century to do penance, working miracles even after death. The grotto is supposed to be the place in Jerusalem where she lived, died, and was buried.

The Jews place here the Tomb of the Prophetess Huldah.[7] It is revered by followers of Judaism, Christianity, and Islam.

[7] II Kings 22:14.

CHURCH OF THE LORD'S PRAYER

He was praying in a certain place, and when he ceased, one of his disciples said to him, "Lord, teach us to pray, as John taught his disciples." And he said to them, "When you pray, say:

"Father, hallowed be thy name. Thy kingdom come. Give us each day our daily bread; and forgive us our sins, for we ourselves forgive every one who is indebted to us; and lead us not into temptation." [8]

———•·•———

Following the path down from the Chapel of the Ascension in the village of Kafr et Tur on the Mount of Olives, one comes to the Church of the Lord's Prayer or Church of the Pater Noster. It stands, according to ancient tradition, where Christ taught His disciples to pray. Here also Peter the Hermit, instigator of the First Crusade, preached a sermon.

The present sanctuary, to which a convent of French Carmelite nuns is attached, was built in 1875 on the ruins of a twelfth century church constructed by Aurelia Bossi, Princess of La Tour d'Auvergne. Her tomb is found here.

The side walls of the cloister, modeled after the celebrated Cemetery of Pisa, are adorned with tablets of the Lord's Prayer in thirty-two different languages. This solemn court is commonly called the Hall of the Lord's Prayer.

During a methodical excavation in 1910–1911, a church was discovered, perfectly orientated, that had three aisles and a crypt with a small apse. The capitals, trunks, and bases of the columns and the mosaics brought to light were ascribed by archaeologists

[8] St. Luke 11:1–4. See also St. Matthew 5:1–2 and 6:9–15.

to the golden period of Empress Helena and her son Constantine the Great. It was undoubtedly here that Empress Helena built the large Church of Eleona, at the same time she built the Church of the Nativity in A.D. 330; and these newly uncovered ruins are the remains of her glorious sanctuary.

THE GARDEN OF GETHSEMANE

And every day he was teaching in the temple, but at night he went out and lodged on the mount called Olivet.[9]

He went forth with his disciples across the Kidron Valley, where there was a garden, which he and his disciples entered.[10]

To a place which was called Gethsemane.[11]

———•——•———

"Hortus Gethsemani" is the inscription cut on a massive stone lintel above the gate leading into the Holy Land's most sacred, solemn, and simple garden. This garden, surrounded by high stone walls, contains a number of ancient and venerable olive trees, most of which are several hundred years old. The oldest, on the south side next to the Basilica of Gethsemane, is known to be at least nine hundred years old and is called the Tree of Agony. The word Gethsemane signifies "oil press." The oil that is pressed from the olives of the Tree of Agony and of the other venerable trees is highly treasured, as are the rosaries made from the olive pits.

In this garden, which belonged to one of the disciples,[12] or in the home of friends in near-by Bethany,[13] Jesus spent the night after a day's teaching in Jerusalem. The New Testament records that after "they had sung a hymn" at the Last Supper [14] Christ

9 St. Luke 21:37.
10 St. John 18:1.
11 St. Mark 14:32.
12 St. Luke 21:37.
13 St. Matthew 21:17.
14 See St. Matthew 26:20–30; St. Mark 14:17–26;
St. Luke 22:14–38; and St. John, Chapters 13–17.

and all the "twelve" but Judas, who had left the Last Supper "after receiving the morsel," [15] went, "as was his custom, to the Mount of Olives." [16] "And they went to a place which was called Gethsemane; and he said to his disciples, 'Sit here, while I pray.' " [17] Christ "took with him Peter and James and John" [18] and "withdrew from them about a stone's throw, and knelt down and prayed." [19] "Now Judas, who betrayed him, also knew the place; for Jesus often met there with his disciples." [20]

"Rise, let us be going; see, my betrayer is at hand," [21] Christ said to his sleeping disciples after his hour of "agony" had passed; "and immediately, while he was still speaking, Judas came, one of the twelve, and with him a crowd with swords and clubs, from the chief priests and the scribes and the elders." [22]

"Now the betrayer had given them a sign, saying, 'The one I shall kiss is the man; seize him and lead him away safely.' " [23] "And he came up to Jesus at once and said, 'Hail, Master!' And he kissed him." [24] "So the band of soldiers and their captain and the officers of the Jews seized Jesus and bound him" [25] "and led him away." [26]

[15] St. John 13:26–30.
[16] St. Luke 22:39.
[17] St. Mark 14:32.
[18] St. Mark 14:33.
[19] St. Luke 22:41.
[20] St. John 18:2.
[21] St. Mark 14:42.
[22] St. Mark 14:43.
[23] St. Mark 14:44.
[24] St. Matthew 26:49.
[25] St. John 18:12.
[26] St. Luke 22:54.

THE BASILICA OF GETHSEMANE

Sit here, while I pray.[27]

Watch and pray that you may not enter into temptation; the spirit indeed is willing, but the flesh is weak.[28]

Father, if thou art willing, remove this cup from me; nevertheless not my will, but thine, be done.[29]

———— • ————

On the southern side of the Garden of Gethsemane stands the majestic Basilica of Gethsemane. The Peregrinatio S. Silviae, a valuable document on the ancient liturgy of Jerusalem, confirmed by the itineraries of the pilgrims in the subsequent centuries, dates the earliest account of the existence of a sanctuary at the foot of the Mount of Olives as the fourth century. It also records that among the various caves in the garden one particular grotto was known under the name of Gethsemane or Oil Press. It was thought the site where Jesus was seized and bound by "the band of soldiers and their captain and the officers of the Jews." [30] But during the fourteenth century a misunderstanding arose among the pilgrims, and the grotto became known as the Grotto of the Agony. "And he withdrew from them about a stone's throw, and knelt down and prayed," we find written in St. Luke 22:41. In verse 45 is recorded, "when he rose from prayer, he came to the disciples and found them sleeping." Tradition points to a large rock—known as the Rock of the Three Apostles—behind the Basilica of Gethsemane as that upon which Peter, James, and John slept during the Master's anguish.

The present Basilica, completed in 1925, very closely follows the limits of the fourth century sanctuary as the ancient foundations were discovered in the preparation of the new. Black marble lines and round figures in the present pavement mark the course

27 St. Mark 14:32.
28 St. Mark 14:38 and St. Matthew 26:41.
29 St. Luke 22:42.
30 St. John 18:12.

of the ancient walls and the places where the old columns stood.

The beautiful façade is mainly of a veined pink limestone in Byzantine style. It consists of a very attractive open portico, fronted with lovely columns of the Corinthian order, placed between three spacious arches. Above the columns and between the arches are placed marble statues of the four Evangelists—Matthew, Mark, Luke, and John. Behind these, up to the pediment, are brilliant designs in colored and gilt mosaics.

The windows on the side of the Basilica are surmounted by sculptured pointed gables and capped with large lion heads. Around the church, above the windows, runs a frieze of carved olive branches with fruit, symbolical of the olive trees in Gethsemane. All the materials and all the workmanship in the church are Palestinian, with the sole exception of the splendidly carved white marble capitals, which are from Italy.

Inside the arches is an open court, on the eastern side of which are the immense bronze doors of the church, flanked on each side by two huge windows of white marble fretwork. The costly glazing is double, and it consists of handsome designs in dark-colored glass, producing the desired effect of quiet and somber lighting. The ceiling of the portico is finished with bronze panels.

The interior of the Basilica is quadrangular with six columns in a double row supporting the roof and dividing the central apse from the two side apses. On the north and the south are four windows similar to those described above. The high altar is of magnificent colored and variegated Palestinian marble, quarried at Beit Sahur, near Bethlehem. The apse above it is adorned with a fine and extensive mosaic of Christ praying, "Let this cup pass from me." Smaller mosaics in the side apses represent, on the right, the arrest of Christ at Gethsemane and, on the left, Christ being led off by "the great crowd with swords and clubs, from the chief priests and the elders of the people." [31]

The central part of the floor of the church is paved with minute polished mosaics in scriptural designs. The mosaics from the

[31] St. Matthew 26:47.

original pavement of the fourth century church have been slightly depressed in this newer pavement.

The interior of the roof of the Basilica consists of twelve low domes, each of which is radiant with a panel in colored and gilt mosaics. The panels, given by various countries, represent twelve principles in the life of Christ: first panel, given by Argentina, Column of the Flagellation; second, given by Chile, St. Veronica's Handkerchief; third, given by Brazil, the Three Spikes; fourth, given by Mexico, the shield of St. Francis; fifth and most important, being right over the Rock of Agony and the high altar, Heaven with Angels, given by Italy; sixth, given by France, the Chalice, symbolic of the Sacrament; seventh, given by Spain, The Holy Cross; eighth, given by England, the Holy Sepulcher; ninth, given by Belgium, the Crown of Thorns; tenth, given by Canada, the One-Piece Garment; eleventh, given by Germany, the Spear and the Sponge; and twelfth, given by the United States, the Crusader Cross of the Holy Land.

"Tarry ye here and watch with me" is the very fitting Latin inscription above the bronze door, and truly a pilgrim finds this Basilica in the Garden of Gethsemane a sacred site for quiet meditation.

BASILICA OF THE AGONY

"Father, if thou art willing, remove this cup from me; nevertheless not my will, but thine, be done." And there appeared to him an angel from heaven, strengthening him. And being in an agony he prayed more earnestly; and his sweat became like great drops of blood falling down upon the ground.[32]

———— ◆ ————

Just opposite the garden gate to the Church of St. Mary Magdalene is a small reddish column built into a wall. Approximately here in the olive grove, according to tradition, "the man called

[32] St. Luke 22:42–44.

Judas, one of the twelve, drew near to Jesus" [33] to betray him with a kiss. The Church of St. Mary Magdalene, built by Czar Alexander III in 1888, is surmounted by beautiful gold-covered domes. It is a living memorial to Mary, called Magdalene, from whom Jesus cast out seven demons; Mary, to whom Jesus first appeared after his resurrection. Behind its altar hangs the most famous oil painting in Palestine—Vereshchagin's "The Angel at the Tomb." Because women are not permitted behind the altar, only men have the privilege of viewing this magnificent painting.

The first known Basilica erected on this spot was built in the time of Theodosius (379–393). Outside the walled city of Jerusalem, it was one of the first Christian sanctuaries to be destroyed by the invading Persians. The following centuries saw it rise and fall again. Upon the arrival of the Crusaders, the native Christians built there a modest chapel, which was enlarged later and named St. Saviour. This church was also destroyed, and services were transferred to a near-by grotto, which tradition since the fourth century had connected with Judas's kiss and Christ's arrest. At the time of the transfer the grotto began to be known as the Grotto of the Agony, or the Rock of Agony.

Archaeological excavations in the garden, which began in 1891 and continued in 1909, uncovered the ruins of the Church of St. Saviour. In 1929, however, while the foundations were being prepared for reconstructing that sanctuary invaluable remains of the Theodosian church came to light, at a lower level.

The New Testament records that the place of Christ's solitary prayer on the Mount of Olives and the place where Judas betrayed his master are but a "stone's throw" apart, and it is easy to understand that through the centuries pilgrims would somewhat alter sites identified earlier.

Still another traditional site, near the Church of the Virgin, is that of Christ's agony. It is a rock-hewn cavern, called the Grotto of the Agony, about fifty-four feet long, twenty-seven feet wide,

[33] St. Luke 22:47.

and twelve feet high. Traces of the ancient frescoes can still be seen on its ceiling, which is borne partly by natural and partly by masonry pillars. It contains three altars and some ancient stone benches. This sanctuary has been maintained by the Franciscans since 1392.

CHURCH OF THE VIRGIN

The angel Gabriel was sent from God to a city of Galilee named Nazareth, to a virgin betrothed to a man whose name was Joseph, of the house of David; and the virgin's name was Mary. And he came to her and said, "Hail, O favored one, the Lord is with you."

"And behold, you will conceive in your womb and bear a son, and you shall call his name Jesus."

And Mary said, "Behold I am the handmaid of the Lord; let it be to me according to your word." [34]

———•——•———

At the foot of the Mount of Olives, a short distance from the Garden of Gethsemane and to the right of the Jericho Road after one has crossed the small Brook of Kidron,[35] is the Church of the Virgin or the Church of the Assumption—in Arabic, Keniset Sitti Miriam. It is also often referred to as the Sarcophagus of Mary. The Roman Catholics name this sanctuary the Tomb of the Blessed Virgin. According to their tradition, Mary was interred in the Tomb of the Blessed Virgin but arose on the "third day" and ascended to heaven, "for not being subject to the yoke of sin she bore not the consequences of sin, which are the corruption of the flesh." This tomb, then, thereafter became the shrine of "her glorious Assumption into Heaven." The sanctuary lies below the level of the road and is approached by a long flight of stone steps. A porch is the only part of the church above the ground level, the church floor being thirty-five feet below it.

[34] St. Luke 1:26-28, 31, 38.
[35] See I Kings 2:37, 15:13; II Kings 23:6; II Chronicles 29:16; Nehemiah 2:15; Jeremiah 31:40; and John 18:1.

Here, according to legend, Mary the mother of Jesus was buried by the Apostles.

The first church on this traditional site, octagonal with a large dome, was erected sometime between 431 and 451. This was destroyed by the Arab invaders in 614, and was later restored; but the Crusaders found it again in ruins. The small edicule over the sepulcher of Mary, however, had been preserved. Godfrey de Bouillon then constructed the Abbey of the Valley of Jehoshaphat, a monastery, near the site for the Benedictines of Cluny; and on them was laid the responsibility for protecting this hallowed ground. The valley in which the monastery was erected is also known as the Kidron Valley, and the Arabs call it Wady Sitti Miriam. It bounds Jerusalem on its entire eastern extent. Because of the accumulation of debris through the centuries, the bottom of the valley now is from ten to fifty feet higher than in biblical times. It also is thirty feet farther east, and the ancient surface of its west side, at the southeast angle of the present city wall, is reached only after going through thirty-six feet of debris. In this valley, at the foot of Ophel, is the only spring of Jerusalem, the Virgin's Fount.

The present church was built in 1161 by Millicent, daughter of King Baldwin II of Jerusalem and wife of Fulk of Anjou, third Latin King of Jerusalem. It has remained standing through the centuries since the return to Jerusalem of the Saracens, who razed to the ground the Benedictine monastery, mainly because Muhammedans held sacred the church constructed over the tomb of Christ's mother.

The Franciscans gained possession of the church in the second half of the fourteenth century and cared for the property until 1757. Since that time the Greek Orthodox Church has been its possessor. However, it has graciously granted the right to hold services in the sanctuary to the Roman Catholics, the Armenians, the Syrians, and the Abyssinians.

The edicule which contains the Tomb of the Blessed Virgin or the Sarcophagus of Mary, rises at the foot of forty-seven marble steps. Two doors, one to the west, the other to the north, lead to the sepulchral chamber where the Virgin is laid. The sarcophagus resembles that of Christ found in the Holy Sepulcher. The tomb is rock-hewn, separated from the surrounding rock for architectural reasons.

South of the chapel containing Mary's tomb is a prayer niche revered by the Moslems. It is here that Caliph Omar is said to have come for special prayers after his capture of the Holy City in 637. To the west of the prayer niche is an altar used by the Greek Orthodox fathers. In an apse at the extreme east is an Armenian altar, and in the opposite, or west, wing is an Abyssinian. Directly in front of the Abyssinian altar is the mouth of a cistern, the water of which is supposed to cure certain diseases.

The church also contains the tombs of Joachim and Anna, the parents of Mary. Early records show that they were buried originally where the Church of St. Anne now stands; but, sometime during the fifteenth century, they were transferred to a small chapel about halfway down the staircase to the church proper. Their tombs occupy the chapel to the right, in which the ashes of Queen Millicent were also deposited in 1161.

In a chapel to the left, directly opposite the tombs of Joachim and Anna, is an altar over the alleged Tomb of Joseph. This church then, according to tradition, contains the tombs of Mary, the mother of Christ; Joseph, her husband; Anna, her mother; and Joachim, her father. The site is sacred to all Christians and to the followers of Islam.

Ascending to the court in front of the church, a passage to the left leads to the Grotto of the Agony.

CHURCH OF ST. ANNE

The Church of St. Anne, a restored Crusader abbey, occupies the site, according to a fourth century tradition, of the home of Joachim and Anna, the parents of the Virgin. One finds this church on the road called Tarik Bab Sitti Miriam, just inside

St. Stephen's Gate—the only gate opening today into the walled city of Jerusalem from the east.

St. Stephen's Gate is so called by Christians because tradition locates here the stoning of Stephen, one of the seven "deacons" in the early church. Acts 7:57–58 records that "they cried out with a loud voice and stopped their ears and rushed together upon him. Then they cast him out of the city and stoned him." Native Christians, however, usually refer to the gate as Bab Sitti Miriam, or the Gate of Our Lady Mary, because it opens toward the Church of the Virgin.

During the time of Christ, the Probatic or Sheep Gate lay in the approximate vicinity of St. Stephen's Gate. It was here that large flocks of sheep were brought to await worshipers who desired to purchase one to sacrifice in the Temple.

The gate also has two other names, one being Bab el Asbat, the Gate of the Tribes. The Jews refer to it as the Gate of Lions, because of the rude sculptures of lions that adorn it.

The Church of St. Anne was erected during the Roman Empire upon the remains of an old fifth or early sixth century shrine. An Arabic inscription on the front of the Crusader church dates from the time of Saladin, who converted it into a Moslem college, and, honoring him, the Arabs call it Salahiya. For nearly seven centuries the Moslems kept possession of this sanctuary; but after the Crimean War the Sultan of Turkey presented it, along with the ruins of the monastery, to the French Government in recognition of the aid rendered. Reconstructed by the architect Mauss, it was placed under the care of the White Fathers and opened to pilgrims in 1878.

The interior of the church is 120 feet long and 66 feet wide. The nave is 42 feet high, but the aisles are only 24 feet. The dome over the transept was probably restored by the Saracens. In the southeastern part of the church a flight of steps descends into a rock-hewn crypt, believed to have been part of the home of Mary's parents and her birthplace. The graves of Joachim and Anna are also shown here.

THE TWIN POOLS OF BETHESDA

Now there is in Jerusalem by the sheep gate a pool, in Hebrew called Bethesda, which has five porticoes. In these lay a multitude of invalids, blind, lame, paralyzed.[36]

———•———

The Twin Pools of Bethesda have been found to the west of the Church of St. Anne. Tradition records that the water of the pools had a supernatural power at certain times, and the first sick person to immerse himself when the "waters were troubled" was miraculously healed. They were naturally surrounded during the day by a great multitude of sick, blind, paralyzed, lame, and withered believers. It was here that Jesus found a man "who had been ill for thirty-eight years." [37] Knowing that the man "had been lying there a long time, he said to him, "Do you want to be healed?" [38] "Sir," the suffering believer answered, "I have no man to put me into the pool when the water is troubled, and while I am going another steps down before me." [39] Then "Jesus said to him, 'Rise, take up your pallet, and walk.' And at once the man was healed, and he took up his pallet and walked." [40]

A gate opposite the Church of St. Anne leads to the excavations of the pools. An enclosed staircase between the street entrance and the church leads down to the southeast corner of the southern pool. The pools are placed north and south and are 164 feet square, 31 feet deep, and are divided by a wall of rock about 20 feet wide. They are cut in the solid rock, with an additional height of three or four courses of masonry wall added. Of each pool all the corners have been discovered except the northwestern, excavations in these parts being impossible because of the buildings above them. There can be no doubt, however, that

[36] St. John 5:2–3.
[37] St. John 5:5.
[38] St. John 5:6.
[39] St. John 5:7.
[40] St. John 5:8–9.

they are the "twin pools" with five porches near the Sheep Gate, where, after the "troubling of the waters," invalids were healed.

The "five porches" mentioned are doubtless the four sides and the middle division. So far no spring of water has been found which could have fed the pools—a mystery yet to be explained. A shaft cut in the rock, with grooves chipped in the sides to enable a man to climb down, leads to a channel below the bottom of the south pool. A trapdoor in the north pool communicates with this duct, which goes southward and can be followed as far as the road in front of the church. The object of this was undoubtedly for cleaning the reservoirs.

The remains of two churches, one built over the ruins of the other, can be seen in the south portion of the north pool. The first is Byzantine and was called St. Maria Probatika as early as 381. It was destroyed, and the Crusaders, who had evidently identified the pools, erected over it a new church, whose crypt was divided into five transverse sections, to represent the porches. This church in turn was destroyed, and the pools covered up. The excavations conducted by the architect Mauss in 1871 and the more recent diggings by the White Fathers have rediscovered these ancient sanctuaries.

THE KING ENTERS JERUSALEM

1

O mighty King, enter riding.
Multitudes sing Thy praise,
Palm branches and rare cloaks
Are spread before Thee.

2

O mighty King, enter riding
In this triumphant procession.
The time has come to be victorious
Over death and evil.

3

O mighty King, enter riding.
Heavenly hosts have come
From high to sing Thy praise,
My Lord, and King of Kings!

PALM SUNDAY IN RAM ALLAH

Behold, there is a feast of the Lord in Shiloh yearly in a place which is on the north side of Bethel, on the east side of the highway that goeth up from Bethel to Shecham, and on the south of Lebonah.

Therefore they commanded the children of Benjamin, saying, Go and lie in wait in the vineyards;

And see, and, behold, if the daughters of Shiloh come out to dance in dances, then come ye out of the vineyards, and catch you every man his wife of the daughters of Shiloh, and go to the land of Benjamin.[41]

———•◆•———

On Palm Sunday afternoon in Ram Allah, a prosperous, healthy, and beautiful Christian Arab village ten miles north of Jerusalem, one can view the reenactment of a portion of Old Testament scripture.[42] In the gayest, most colorful and elaborately cross-stitched native costumes, young unwed Christian maidens of the village gather to dance traditional Palm Sunday folk dances on the smooth-surfaced village threshing floor. Even the smallest lass borrows a costume, not to be outdone by her older sisters, and joins the joyous fête.

Crowds of men, young and old, circle the threshing floor to observe the festivities and speculate on the desirability of the most graceful and comely dancers.

Peddlers find the excited dancers and the enthusiastic observers easy prey for cold refreshments, special sweets, and cakes. For-

41 Judges 21:19–21.
42 Judges 21:16–23.

tune tellers increase their fortunes fast during the festival by encouraging hungry-eyed youths to look into the future where every "Benjaminite has a bashful bride."

The reenacted drama does not reach the spirited climax of the original setting, however, for modern youth, though seemingly eager, dare not carry off the maidens of their choice as did the Benjaminites of old.

ARRAYYANEH *

1

Arrayyaneh, Arrayyaneh
Meat and rice and pine seeds too.
O Nuha, ask God
To fill your house with healthy boys.

2

Lots of rice, lots of rice,
O precious cooks of rice today.
God be with you, God be with you,
All who helped against our foes.

* *Arrayyaneh* is a typical Arabian nonsense word. This selection is a typical Palm Sunday *Sihsaleh*, or Ram Allah women's dance. The dancers line up in two rows, facing each other. One group sings and dances forward towards the other. The dancers' hands are on one another's shoulders. As the first group dances back to its original position, the second group sings and moves forward. This continues indefinitely. The above words are merely typical ones recorded in 1944. Hundreds and hundreds of original verses are sung before the celebration ends.

3

Walk slowly beside the spring.
Walk slowly beside the spring.
Basim called to his loved one.
Answered she, "Yes, my eyes!"

ALIMWAIL *

1

Alimwail, Alimwail, Alimwail lalyya!
What a crowd of horsemen coming in the evening!
Meet them, Abu Yusuf—a thousand and a hundred,
Armed with glittering swords, horses wet with perspiration!
Do not let them catch your maidens.

2

Alimwail, Alimwail, Alimwail lalyya!
What a crowd of horsemen coming in the night!
Meet them, Abu Fuad, meet them and their horses,
Armed with daggers shining, horses prancing, even wet with per-
     spiration!
Abu, Abu do not let them steal your daughters.†

* An Arabian nonsense word. This is another famous *Sihsaleh*.
† In every verse a different Abu, father, is named. The men named by the
women in this dance are tribe favorites, loved and respected by all.

CHAPTER VII

Foot-Washing Thursday

Now before the feast of the Passover, when Jesus knew that his hour had come to depart out of this world to the Father, having loved his own who were in the world, he loved them to the end.[1]

Jesus . . . rose from supper, laid aside his garments, and girded himself with a towel. Then he poured water into a basin, and began to wash the disciples' feet, and to wipe them with a towel with which he was girded.[2]

———•———

JUST as Christ washed the feet of his disciples after the Last Supper, teaching that "a servant is not greater than his master; nor is he who is sent greater than he who sent him," [3] the Greek Orthodox Patriarch annually emphasizes the Master's lesson by publicly washing the feet of twelve of his church subordinates in the presence of his Christian subjects. As Christ so solemnly and sincerely impressed upon the minds of the disciples, the Patriarch, seeking to impress present-day Christians, repeats Christ's words: " 'You call me Teacher and Lord; and you are right, for so I am. If I then, your Lord and Teacher, have washed your feet, you also ought to wash one another's feet. For I have given you an example, that you also should do as I have done to you.' " [4]

Hundreds and hundreds of Greek Orthodox pilgrims gather in the courtyard of the Church of the Holy Sepulcher at high

[1] St. John 13:1.
[2] St. John 13:3–5.
[3] St. John 13:16.
[4] St. John 13:13–15.

noon on Passion Week Thursday. A platform, previously erected
in the courtyard, is high enough for all pilgrims to watch the
impressive reenactment of a scene lifted direct from the events
of the Last Supper. In this, unlike other Christian feasts and
festivities, the pilgrims are very quiet, patient, expectant and
converse only in hushed tones. No singing or chanting or dancing takes place at this grave ceremony. The colorfully costumed
Patriarch and twelve of his "disciples" are unceremoniously directed through the waiting mob and ascend the richly bedecked
platform. The "disciples" sit, and the drama begins.

The Patriarch lays "aside his garments, and [girds] himself
with a towel. Then he [pours] water into a basin, and [begins]
to wash the disciples' feet, and to wipe them with the towel with
which he [is] girded." Actually, the Patriarch washes only one
foot of each priest. When the Patriarch comes to the priest representing Simon Peter, Peter says to him, "Lord, do you wash my
feet?" And in the words of Christ, the Patriarch answers him
saying, "What I am doing you do not know now, but afterward
you will understand." Then Peter says to him, "You shall never
wash my feet," and the Patriarch answers as of old, "If I do not
wash you, you have no part in me." "Lord, not my feet only,"
cries Peter, "but also my hands and my head." "He who has
bathed does not need to wash, except for his feet," is the response, "but he is clean all over; and you are clean." [5]

The basin of water used for this archaic ceremony is then taken
into the Church of the Holy Sepulcher, blessed, and made available for the pilgrims. In a slow and endless procession the pilgrims
pass by the Holy Water to dip and sanctify very small cloth bags
of delicate bark in the precious water. The bags are reverently
carried home, permitted to dry, then safely stowed away to be
used later as incense to drive away family illness. When this hallowed bark is burnt with alum (potassium aluminum sulphate),
according to tradition, it will drive away the "evil eye."

Foot-Washing Thursday (*Khamis al-ghusul* in Arabic) is a

[5] St. John 13:4–11.

Greek Orthodox Church ceremony only. The Protestants in the Holy Land climb the Mount of Olives to the Garden of Gethsemane on Passion Week Thursday and hold a service of hymns and prayers.

CHAPTER VIII

The Holy Fire Ceremony

We laud the Holy Fire,
We visit our Lord's Tomb;
Our Lord is Jesus the Christ
He who came into this world
And bought us with His holy blood.
Today we rejoice; the Jews are sad;
There is no religion
But the religion of Christ!

IN DIRECT contrast to the solemn ceremony on Foot-Washing Thursday, is the hilarious, boisterous, uncontrolled festival, called simply the Holy Fire ceremony, that takes place on Saturday before Easter. This is a must for the folk specialist looking for the most complicated folk dances and elaborate costumes of the Arab world. According to the tradition of the Greek Orthodox Church, fire from heaven spontaneously bursts forth annually from the Tomb of Christ on the day before Easter. It is always "received" by the Patriarch alone in the Tomb, and brought by him as a blessed token and reminder of God's might.

Undoubtedly the Western custom of appearing on Easter Day in newly purchased and styled apparel comes direct from this antiquated Greek Orthodox Church ceremony where every man, woman, and child comes to the gala fête wearing the most picturesque and newest and most exquisite costume possible to purchase or make.

The merry laughter is infectious, the fiery dancing is intriguing, the singing enchanting, and the chanting hypnotic. Laughter and dancing and chanting and singing, mixed with spe-

76

cial Easter cakes, candy, bitter Arab coffee, and Holy Land wine, really furnish the ingredients for an unusual, if not majestic, celebration.

Dancing begins about midmorning in the *manara* immediately outside the walled city's New Gate. Christian pilgrims arrive from every district of the Holy Land to take an active part in the time-honored Jerusalem procession and festivities. People also come from Egypt, Syria, Lebanon, and many other countries. Moslem villagers also often join in the dancing and singing of this joyous celebration.

Late arrivals swarm the *manara* in search of their village or tribe circles. Within each village circle the heads of families or tribes have bright-colored church and family banners much in evidence. Each circle has a number of sets of folk dancers in full sway doing their special village version of the *debki,* the national Arab men's dance. The dance leaders display their most intricate steps and chant their most unique poetry on this occasion, and the sword dancers make every effort to display their dexterity and superior talents.

By high noon the dancers and singers and onlookers have reached a feverish pitch of excitement, and the carefully timed arrival of the Patriarch and his retinue brings forth a most spontaneous and exhilarating greeting. The dancers begin the parade into the walled city and are followed immediately by the priests and the Patriarch. Only men are permitted to take an active part in the formal parade, the chanting and dancing. The chanters or "prayer men " are next in the procession with their lanterns. The heads of Christian families follow with gaudy banners waving, and the bold mob sweeps alongside and behind the formal train. On through the walled city the mass moves, past hundreds of observers perched on roof tops and on gaily decorated balconies, and to the Church of the Holy Sepulcher.

Upon arrival at the church, the priests and the Patriarch and the formal parade participants enter to continue the Call for Holy Fire. The dancers and the general mass of pilgrims remain in the courtyard of the church to continue their merry-making, for soon after the early morning opening of the doors the interior of the church was filled to capacity with celebrants. The Patriarch enters the Tomb of Christ alone as his subordinates remain in the outer sanctuary in concentrated prayer. Around and around and around the Tomb the procession moves, and the Christian chanting rolls, lifts, and falls like heavenly thunder. The nonparticipating pilgrims remain in hushed suspense until at long last the Patriarch is seen to emerge from the Tomb with a lighted torch of Holy Fire sent direct from God. The old Greek Orthodox Christians believe that the Holy Fire will not burn. They put their hands on it, then their faces, and bring the children also to receive the sacred blessing. Often vows are made to keep the fire lit in the home for the entire year. A special pottery oil lamp is provided for the Holy Fire, and the lighted lamp is placed directly below a picture of Christ or St. Mary.

The scene that follows the Patriarch's appearance is beyond human description. The uncontrolled response of the mob surges the entire sea of human bodies forward toward the Patriarch and the Holy Fire. He is hurriedly and almost madly raised to the shoulders of his subordinates to save him from being crushed and smothered in the hysterical rush forward to secure a light from the fire sent direct from heaven. It is only a matter of minutes before thousands and thousands of torches and candles and lanterns are lighted, clothes catch fire and are smothered out, pilgrims are trampled over, fights start, chanting becomes piercing screams, and the heated air becomes nauseating. The smell of countless sweating human bodies, mingled with burning incense and tallow, excitement and previously taken spirits overcomes many a pilgrim.

Once out in the fresh air with vomiting over, that inhuman soul known as a folklore specialist will need to rush for the nearest travel conveyance in order to dash to a near-by Christian village to see the continuation of this holy celebration.

Back in the Christian village of Ram Allah, a typical Christian village near Jerusalem, the majority of the townsfolk, old men, most women and children, eagerly await the arrival of the Holy Fire at the village *manara*. Young men take pleasure in running races from the Tomb to the village with the precious fire, for it is indeed an honor to bring a gift to the village direct from heaven. At one time the races took place on horseback, but to-day taxis and busses are used. At the first sight of the Fire the eager inhabitants break into shrill shouts and songs and prayers and dances. Immediately upon the arrival of the village priest and the heads of the families, the villagers repeat the colorful Holy City procession and parade with much rejoicing, lighted candles in hand, to their local church for mass.

Following the special mass, the village women return home to prepare the year's most bountiful feast. For forty days the strict Christian has fasted without meat or anything produced by fowl or beast. Lamb and fowl and rice and eggs and cheese and vegetables and sweets—all will be abundantly prepared for tribe feasting.

All through the night and on into Easter Day the men carry the "light" and intone the Holy Fire Chant through the village streets, at the doors of relatives and friends, and at the Guest House and Church. Patriotic songs are also included in the light-hearted singing and spirited dancing.

HOLY FIRE CHANT

1

We feast the Holy Fire.
We come to our Lord's Tomb.
Our Lord is Jesus Christ.
He came to this sad earth.

2

Christ bought us with His blood.
Today we can rejoice.

The house of Israel mourns.
We worship but the Christ!

3

We feast the Holy Fire
When Christ rose from the dead.
The tomb was torn asunder
And holy fire appeared.

ST. GEORGE'S CHANT

With candles in our hands
We kneel around Thy tomb;
To thee, St. George, we pray
For continued Christian love.

CHAPTER IX

The Easter Pilgrimage

IN THE Western world, Christmas is the most colorful, talked-about, and planned-for holiday of the entire year. In the Near East, home of Christmas and Christianity, however, Easter is the holiday of holidays. True, it has its period of deepest sorrow and distress during the time of Christ's agony on the Mount of Olives, at his betrayal and trial and conviction and crucifixion. But did not Christ conquer the world? Did he not rise and enter into the kingdom of heaven? "Christ arose," is the happy Easter morning greeting in the Holy Land. "Truly, he is risen," is the jubilant reply.

In Jerusalem, Bethlehem, Nazareth, Ram Allah, and other Christian centers of the Holy Land, the midnight service on Easter Eve fills the churches and streets with rejoicing Christians. The jubilant ceremonies continue throughout the night and into the dawn of Easter. Before sunrise, sleepers are aroused by the rhythmic chanting and loud shouting of men marching in the streets with lighted torches.

"We feast, behold the Holy Fire," they chant as they pay respect to the priests and at the village guest houses. "Christ is risen!" and "May you be well and strong throughout the year!" are the traditional greetings. "Truly, he is risen!" and "Every year may you be well!" are the traditional responses.

Easter is truly a New Year's Day to the Holy Land Christians, who spend the entire day, after attending at least one church service, in visiting and greeting old and new friends and relatives. To children it is filled with excitement and adventure, for they travel from door to door announcing the resurrection of Christ and receive in return hard-boiled colored Easter eggs. Children have been known to return home with more than three dozen eggs.

The pilgrim in search of living folk-drama, so filled with tradition and pageantry, becomes slightly frustrated during the great Passion Week in Palestine. Biblical history pushes out the present in its annual rebirth, and the pilgrim becomes an actor of the past in the world's most powerful drama. Within the span of seven suns the actors relive scenes of Victory and Love and Despair and Hate and Agony and Injustice and Tragedy and Death and Resurrection.

VIA DOLOROSA [1]

"Away with him, away with him, crucify him!" [2]

"Why, what evil has he done? I have found in him no crime deserving death; I will therefore chastise him and release him."
But they were urgent, demanding with loud cries that he should be crucified. And their voices prevailed. So Pilate gave sentence that their demand should be granted. [3]

And they clothed him in a purple cloak, and plaiting a crown of thorns they put it on him. And they began to salute him, "Hail, King of the Jews!" And they struck his head with a reed, and spat upon him, and they knelt down in homage to him. And when they had mocked him, they stripped him of the purple cloak, and put his own clothes on him. And they led him out to crucify him. [4]

Two others also, who were criminals, were led away to be put to death with him. And when they came to the place which is called the Skull, there they crucified him, and the criminals, one on the right and one on the left.

[1] The complete biblical descriptions covering the period between Christ's arrest in the Garden of Gethsemane and his burial in the rock-hewn tomb can be found in St. Matthew 26:57–75, 27:1–66; St. Mark 14:53–72, 15:1–47; St. Luke 22:54–71, 23:1–56; and St. John 18:12–40, 19:1–42.
[2] St. John 19:15.
[3] St. Luke 23:22–24.
[4] St. Mark 15:17–20.

And Jesus said, "Father, forgive them; for they know not what they do." [5]

Then Jesus, crying with a loud voice, said, "Father, into thy hands I commit my spirit!"
And having said this he breathed his last. [6]

. . . Joseph from the Jewish town of Arimathea . . . took the body, and wrapped it in a clean linen shroud, and laid it in his own new tomb, which he had hewn in the rock; and he rolled a great stone to the entrance of the tomb, and departed.

And Mary Magdalene and the other Mary were there, sitting opposite the tomb. [7]

———•———

The Via Dolorosa begins, according to established tradition, from the former courtyard of the Praetorium, where the Roman Procurator, Pontius Pilate, had his Jerusalem residence during Jewish Passover. By the Via Dolorosa, or Way of the Cross, is meant the road taken by Christ from his trial at the Praetorium to Calvary. There are fourteen "stations," marked by tablets with numbers or inscriptions, representing scenes enacted along the tragic path. Some stations are mentioned in the Gospels while others are established by ancient tradition.

It was at the Praetorium that Pilate "sat down on the judgment seat at a place called the Pavement" [8] and enacted the mock-trial of Jesus; it was here that Pilate reluctantly and fearfully gave way to the demands of the shouting mob of angry Jews. "Crucify him, crucify him!" rang the cries of the chief priests and officers. "Take him yourselves and crucify him, for I find no crime in him," Pilate replied. And, "wishing to satisfy the crowd," he "delivered him to be crucified." [9] Today this site is occupied by the Convent of the Sisters of Zion. It would interest the pilgrim to know that under the present convent are several sub-

[5] St. Luke 23:32–34.
[6] St. Luke 23:46.
[7] St. Matthew 27:57–61.
[8] St. John 19:13.
[9] St. Mark 15:15.

terranean vaults or passageways communicating with the Temple area. These were probably secret entrances used by the Roman governors in emergencies.

Scholars disagree as to the location of the Praetorium at the time of Christ's trial. Christian tradition, however, places it within the fortress of Antonia. Although the Procurator's ordinary place of residence was Caesarea, it was necessary that he make occasional visits to Jerusalem, where he usually resided at the palace of the dethroned Herods; but, on the occasion of the Jewish Passover, he transferred his residence to the fortress of Antonia so that he might more easily quell the riots of the Jews, so common around the Temple at festival times. Historians assert that, wherever the Procurator fixed his residence, there also was the Praetorium.

The fortress of Antonia, at the northwest of the Temple, existed as early as the time of Jeremiah, when it was known as the Tower of Hananeel.[10] The Maccabees later restored it and named it Baris. It was enlarged and embellished by Herod the Great, who named it Antonia in honor of his friend Mark Antony. The fortress was dismantled by Titus' soldiers in A.D. 70.

Recent excavations by the Franciscans in the Chapel of the Condemnation and the Convent of the Sisters of Zion make visible the heavy Roman pavement of large flags, many of them striated with transverse fluting to prevent horses from slipping. The ancient pavement is several feet below the level of the present road. Traces of games, common among the Roman soldiers, are carved on the flagstones, and at regular intervals are canals undoubtedly made to collect rain water and carry it to the big subterranean cistern beneath.

FIRST STATION

So when Pilate saw that he was gaining nothing, but rather that a riot was beginning, he took water and washed his hands before the

[10] Nehemiah 3:1 and 12:39.

crowd, saying, "I am innocent of this man's blood; see to it yourselves."
And all the people answered, "His blood be on us and on our children!" [11]

———•———

Although Jesus heard the sentence of death pronounced in
the Lithostroton (that is, Pavement), the large court on the west
of the fortress of Antonia, custom starts the Way of the Cross
from the courtyard marked by tradition as the site of Pilate's
palace, in which the interrogation of Christ took place. Within
the palace, Pilate sought to understand on what grounds Christ
was guilty of stirring up such hatred and envy in the chief priests
and the elders. In the near-by barracks, where the Franciscan
Convent of the Flagellation now stands, Christ was taken by
the governor's soldiers following his deliverance to the people,
stripped, dressed in a scarlet robe,[12] crowned with a crown of
thorns, given a reed in imitation of a scepter, mocked, spat upon,
scourged, and with sneers and boisterous laughter proclaimed
King of the Jews.

Within the Franciscan Convent enclosure is the Chapel of the
Flagellation. Important remains of a medieval chapel are still
preserved. Once a stable, then a weaver's workshop, it was almost
reduced to a heap of ruins when Ibrahim Pasha returned it to
the Franciscans in 1838. Maxmilian, the Duke of Bavaria, granted
the necessary funds for its restoration. In 1927 it was completely
renovated in the style of the twelfth century by the architect
A. Barluzzi. The chapel contains three beautiful windows, designed by D. Cambellotti and executed by L. Bicchiarini. They
represent the Flagellation, Pilate washing his hands, and the
triumph of Barabbas, the notorious prisoner and murderer who
received his freedom from Pilate in accordance with the wishes
of the Jewish mob and the established custom of releasing one
prisoner annually at the feast of the Passover.

[11] St. Matthew 27:24–25.
[12] Revised Edition, St. Matthew 27:28. See St. Mark 15:17 and St. John 19:2 for
contradictions.

SECOND STATION

And when they had mocked him, they stripped him of the robe, and put his own clothes on him, and led him away to crucify him.[13]

. . . he went out, bearing his own cross . . .[14]

———•◦•———

The Second Station, signifying where the Cross was laid upon Christ, is below the steps to the barracks and opposite the Chapel of the Condemnation. The chapel stands on the Lithostroton and is a perfect square with the apse to the east. It was reconstructed in the classic style in 1900.

One then passes under the ancient Roman triumphal arch, now called the Ecce Homo Arch from Pilate's statement, "Behold the man!" A tradition of the fifteenth century alleges that the arch marks the spot where "Jesus came out, wearing the crown of thorns and the purple robe" and where "Pilate said to them, 'Here is the man!' " [15] Like other triumphal arches, it is triple, the main vault standing over the road, while the northern arch is seen in the choir of the beautiful church of the Sisters of Zion. The southern arch has disappeared. The whole is thought by some authorities to be the work of Hadrian in A.D. 135 and not one dating from the time of Christ. If it had stood then, it would undoubtedly have been demolished in the general destruction ordered by Titus in A.D. 70.

THIRD STATION

Beyond the Ecce Homo Arch, one passes a Greek Orthodox hospice under which are shown the continuation of the ancient pavement and some rock-hewn chambers which probably formed part of the Roman dungeon in the Antonia. Here the Via Do-

[13] St. Matthew 27:31.
[14] St. John 19:17.
[15] St. John 19:5.

lorosa descends to the junction with the **Damascus Gate** Road, in the Tyropœon valley. The Tyropœon, or central, valley is historically one of the most important of the natural features of Jerusalem and has suffered most from the manifold wreckage and debris of the city. In ancient times it formed a distinct division between the eastern and western Hills; but it has become choked with the waste of centuries, twenty and ninety feet of debris overlying its ancient surface. In ancient times the valley was spanned by two great bridges—one now known as Robinson's Arch—connecting the upper city with the Temple Hill. The valley traverses the whole city, and in its bed is the road from Damascus Gate to Dung Gate.

The pilgrim has now arrived at the point where the Via Dolorosa and the Damascus Gate Road meet. At the corner on the right is the Hospice of the Austrian Pilgrims, and on the left is the Hospice of the United Armenians. Preserved in the Armenian Hospice, in the Church of Notre Dame du Spasme, is a beautiful ancient mosaic pavement.

Outside the Armenian Hospice is a cracked column in the wall which marks the Third Station of the Cross. The Gospel speaks neither of this nor of other falls of Jesus along the Via Dolorosa, but tradition has preserved their memory.

FOURTH STATION

A few steps to the south of Station Three on the Way of the Cross is a second slab in the Armenian Hospice wall, marking the traditional spot where Christ, burdened with the Cross, met Mary, his mother. An undated sanctuary arose here "in perpetual memory of the meeting" and was called the Church of the Spasm, or St. Mary of the Spasm. The Armenian Hospice now on the site is named the Church of Notre Dame du Spasme. The mosaic pavement mentioned contains a representation of two feet which are supposed to indicate the spot where Mary stood when her son passed on the way to Golgotha.

FIFTH STATION

And they compelled a passer-by, Simon of Cyrene, who was coming in from the country, the father of Alexander and Rufus, to carry his cross.[16]

———◆•———

A little Franciscan chapel at the corner of the street marks the Fifth Station. Here Simon the Cyrenian took the Cross from Christ. The commemorative chapel preserves the most ancient record of a convent of the Franciscans in Jerusalem, a sanctuary constructed in the thirteenth century.

SIXTH STATION

Station Six is only a few hundred feet from Station Five. Here, according to tradition, the pious lady Veronica, seeing Jesus pass her house, weighed down with the Cross, pushed her way through the triumphant, hostile, and menacing mob, and wiped the perspiration and blood from her Lord's brow with her handkerchief. Tradition relates that the courageous and kindly woman was compensated in an extraordinary manner, for when she withdrew her handkerchief it bore the impress of his august features.

A recently restored chapel of the Greek Catholics stands to the left, constructed on the site occupied by the house and tomb of Veronica.

SEVENTH STATION

A little beyond Station Six, one crosses the street Bab Khan ez Zeit, and here is the Seventh Station, called Porta Judicaria, or Gate of Judgment. Through this gate Christ is said to have left the city; and here, tradition relates, he fell a second time under the weight of the Cross.

[16] St. Mark 15:21. Also refer to St. Luke 23:26.

At the site of this ancient gate a little Franciscan chapel commemorates Christ's passing.

EIGHTH STATION

And there followed him a great multitude of the people, and of women who bewailed and lamented him. But Jesus turning to them said, "Daughters of Jerusalem, do not weep for me, but weep for yourselves and for your children. For behold, the days are coming when they will say, 'Blessed are the barren, and the wombs that never bore, and the breasts that never gave suck!' Then they will begin to say to the mountains, 'Fall on us'; and to the hills, 'Cover us.' For if they do this when the wood is green, what will happen when it is dry?" [17]

NINTH STATION

Were it possible to proceed directly from Station Eight to Station Nine, the two would be very close indeed; but the Greek Convent of St. Kharalambos has been constructed over the site of the original path, so that it is necessary to retrace our steps to arrive at the next traditional station. This is indicated by a column enclosed in the pillar of the door of the Coptic Monastery, east of the Church of the Holy Sepulcher. Tradition tells us that the weight of the Cross caused Christ to fall here a third time.

ADDITIONAL STATIONS

The Via Dolorosa proper comes to an end at Station Nine. However, the Tenth, Eleventh, Twelfth, and Thirteenth Stations are on Golgotha in the Church of the Holy Sepulcher. At Station Thirteen, as Christ hung from the Cross, he "saw his mother, and the disciple whom he loved standing near." [18] Jesus then said to his mother, "Woman behold your son!" Then he said

---

[17] St. Luke 23:27–31.
[18] St. John 19:26.

to the disciple, "Behold your mother!" "And from that hour the disciple took her to his own home." [19]

After this Jesus, knowing that all was now finished, said (to fulfill the scripture), "I thirst." A bowl full of sour wine stood there; so they put a sponge full of the wine on hyssop and held it to his mouth. When Jesus had received the wine, he said, "It is finished"; and he bowed his head and gave up his spirit.[20]

Station Fourteen is the Holy Sepulcher itself.

. . . Joseph of Arimathea, who was a disciple of Jesus, . . . asked Pilate that he might take away the body of Jesus; and Pilate gave him leave. So he came and took away his body. Nicodemus also, who had at first come to him by night, came bringing a mixture of myrrh and aloes, about a hundred pounds weight. They took the body of Jesus, and bound it in linen cloths with the spices, as is the burial custom of the Jews. Now in the place where he was crucified there was a garden, and in the garden a new tomb where no one had ever been laid. So because of the Jewish day of Preparation, as the tomb was close at hand, they laid Jesus there.[21]

[19] St. John 19:26–27.
[20] St. John 19:28–30.
[21] St. John 19:38–42.

THE CHURCH OF THE HOLY SEPULCHER

Joseph of Arimathea, a respected member of the council, who was also himself looking for the Kingdom of God, took courage and went to Pilate, and asked for the body of Jesus.[22]

22 St. Mark 15:43.

. . . and Pilate gave him leave.[23]

And Joseph took the body, and wrapped it in a clean linen shroud, and laid it in his own new tomb, which he had hewn in the rocks; and he rolled a great stone to the entrance of the tomb, and departed. And Mary Magdalene and the other Mary were there, sitting opposite the tomb.[24]

———•———

Today, as a result of the monumental edifices which the piety of pilgrims has caused to be raised during the centuries, one cannot see Golgotha and the Garden Tomb as they were on the day of Christ's crucifixion. One can, however, look upon the remains of a time-honored stone church that has suffered more brutal attacks and passionate destruction than any other sacred structure.

Since about A.D. 325 the Church of the Holy Sepulcher has been identified by Christians as the holiest spot on earth. Eusebius, in the early part of the fourth century, wrote that Bishop Macarius of Jerusalem, under orders of Constantine the Great, searched the city of Jerusalem and found the Tomb of Christ and Golgotha in that year under the terrace of a pagan temple, which had been erected a century after Christ's crucifixion under the direction of Emperor Hadrian, who made every effort to crush Christianity and obliterate its sites. Hadrian's temple, in reality, preserved this holy site from early destruction.

At this time Empress Helena and her son, Constantine the Great, erected the first sanctuaries, the Church of the Anastasis and the Church of the Martyrium, over what were considered to be the authentic sites of Golgotha and the garden containing the Tomb of Christ. Of these original sanctuaries, scarcely a stone remains today. Tradition also has it that Empress Helena and Constantine discovered the Cross of Christ. Many elderly Christians in the Holy Land today own what they believe to be small bits of the wooden cross. These are usually placed in a beautiful locket and worn to ward off sickness and evil.

[23] St. John 19:38.
[24] St. Matthew 27:59–61.

From east to west, the first sanctuaries were made up of an atrium; a basilica called the Martyrium, constructed on the site where Helena, visiting Jerusalem in 326, found the three crosses of Golgotha; a magnificent cloister, at whose southeast angle rose the bare "stone" of Golgotha; and a beautiful circular church, the Anastasis or Resurrection, in whose center stood a huge rock containing the garden tomb of the risen Christ. Three sides of the rock, for architectural reasons, had been chiseled away and separated from the stone hillside of which it originally formed a part. The vestibule, which stood before the tomb proper, was also removed.

The authenticity of these sites has been long disputed among biblical archaeologists. Later another Golgotha and another Tomb of Christ will be briefly discussed. The sole support of the theory that the Church of the Holy Sepulcher is the true site is the fact that the first Christian Emperor and his mother located it here about 325 after considerable search and the destruction of Hadrian's pagan temple. If the site had not been a venerable one the non-Christians would undoubtedly not have been so thorough in their camouflage.

On the other hand, the city of Jerusalem had been completely destroyed twice during the three hundred years since the Crucifixion, and no document written in that period mentioning the site has yet been disclosed, so that there is room for all to question the site selected by Constantine.

Another point objected to by those who would disprove the authenticity of the site, is that of the course of the "second" north city wall, the determination of which would effectively resolve the doubt as to the Holy Sepulcher, because the Crucifixion as well as the tomb must unquestionably have been outside the city walls. This part of the north wall, all authorities agree, must have passed near the present church; but they disagree as to whether the church would be inside or outside.

However, whether the Church of the Holy Sepulcher stands on the true site or not, this sanctuary, originally built by Constantine, was the prime objective of all the Crusades; and for centuries it has drawn countless pilgrims.

In 614 the Persians under Chosroes (Khosrau) II, with the help of countless Jews, completely demolished Constantine's edifices. Chosroes, who was King of Persia from 590 to 628, invaded and conquered Syria in 611 and Palestine in 614.

In 616–626 Abbot Modestus erected a new set of buildings on a much smaller scale: the Church of the Resurrection, or the Rotunda; the Church of the Cross, over the site of the present Chapel of St. Helena; the Church of Calvary, on the present site; and the Church of the Virgin, which probably stood on the spot now occupied by the great bell tower and the south transept.

When in 637 Jerusalem opened its gates to the Muhammedan conqueror Caliph Omar I, he generously left the Christians in peaceable possession of their churches. Among the presents that the Caliph Harun al-Rashid, of Arabian Nights' celebrity, sent in 800 to Charlemagne were the keys to the Church of the Holy Sepulcher. Charlemagne took advantage of the favorable political relations between himself and the Oriental ruler to establish a hospice on a site southeast of the Church.

Charlemagne, King of the Franks, was the first sovereign of the Christian Empire of the West. He was the first to make a systematic effort at a real restoration of learning in the "Benedictine Age" of learning. He believed in a systematic promotion of clerical education and fostered teaching in both cathedrals and monasteries. In his interest in church music and solicitude for its propagation and adequate performance throughout his empire, he has never been equaled by any civil ruler. The keynote of his legislation, on every point regarding the liturgy, was conformity with Rome.

The reign of Harun al-Rashid (Aaron the Just) ushered in the most brilliant period of Saracenic rule in Asia. The stories of the Arabian Nights have lent a fascination to the name of the remarkable Caliph who was wont to roam the streets of Baghdad by night to remedy injustice, and to relieve the oppressed and destitute. The real man, however, stripped of all the glamour of romance, deserves well the admiration of posterity as indisputably one of the greatest rulers of the world. Faithful in the observance of his religious duties, abstemious in his life, unostentatiously pious and charitable, and yet fond of the pomp and insignia of grandeur, he impressed his personality on popular imagination, and exercised a great influence by his character on society. A soldier by instinct and training, he repeatedly took the field himself; he never spared himself trouble or labor in the work of governing. The perfect immunity from danger with which traders, merchants, scholars, and pilgrims journeyed through the vast empire testifies to the excellence and vigor of his administration. The mosques, colleges and schools, hospitals, dispensaries, caravanserais, roads, bridges, and canals with which he covered the countries under his sway speak of his lively interest in the welfare of his people. During his reign there was general prosperity, and unprecedented progress in the arts and civilization.

In 791, under the pressure of the Empress Zubaida and her brother Isa bin Jaafar, backed by the entire Abbasside clan, Harun nominated his son Muhammed, only five years of age, to succeed him in the Caliphate. Seven years later another son, Abdullah, was made heir presumptive, and it was directed that the throne should go to him on the demise of Muhammed al-Amin. Abdullah received the title al-Ma'mun, the Trusted.

Amin died in 813, after a troublous reign of four years and eight months, at the hand of Persian soldiers. Next morning the assassins exhibited the head of the hapless victim on the walls of Baghdad.

Ma'mun assumed the title of Commander of the Faithful, and the whole of Persia accepted him as Caliph. His receptive mind imbibed and assimilated knowledge that was imparted to him. He was a jurist and a philosopher and knew the Koran by rote, and excelled in its interpretation. His noblemen were treated with consideration and generosity.

Ma'mun, born on the very day Harun, his father, ascended the throne, himself reigned twenty years and six months. He was the most distinguished member of the House of Abbas for prudence, determination, clemency and judgment, sagacity and awe-inspiring aspect, intrepidity, majesty, and liberality. Of that house none wiser than he ever held the Caliphate.

Ma'mun's Caliphate constitutes the most glorious epoch in Saracenic history, and has been justly called the Augustan Age of Islam. It left enduring monuments of the intellectual development of the Moslems in all directions of thought. Its intellectual heritage passed both into Saracenic Spain and into the Christian Constantinople. Ma'mun considered that the true happiness of his people consisted in education and culture.

In sagacious tolerance, Ma'mun recognized no distinction of creed or race; every religious distinction was effaced.

Under Ma'mun, the liberality toward other religions was large-hearted and exemplary. The Patriarchs of Jerusalem and Antioch were the heads of the Christian Church. They retained the privileges and immunities they had enjoyed under sovereigns of their own creed.

Ma'mun was attacked with violent fever in the year 833 and was taken to Tarsus, where he died and was buried in the gardens of a faithful servant of his father. With the last breath of life Ma'mun enjoined his brother and successor, Mustasim, carefully to guard the interests of his subjects, to protect them from oppression, to do justice, and never to transgress the law in the punishment of offenses.

In Ma'mun's reign, about the year 820, the dome of the Church of the Anastasis was enlarged by the Patriarch Thomas. In 935 Ikshhid, a Turk in control of the government of Egypt and Syria, burned the churches and sixty-one years later the mad al-Hakim of the Fatimite dynasty completed the destruction of the ruins left from Ikshhid's burning. Vain attempts to destroy the Tomb itself were made. It was not until 1037 that a new Church of the Holy Sepulcher was completed by the Greek Emperor Michael IV. Only the Church of the Anastasis regained its former magnificence, however, the other venerable spots being marked merely by small oratories. Michael IV was raised to the throne by Empress Zoë, who married him. He died in 1041.

About the beginning of the twelfth century, the Crusaders, thinking the existing sanctuaries too scattered and insignificant, erected a large church in the Romanesque style, which embraced under one roof all the holy places and chapels. It had the form of a cross; but the two transepts were not of equal proportions, as the architects, wishing to retain as much of the aged sanctuaries as possible, retained the portico of the old cloister, known as the Arches of the Virgin, in the northern transept and the Chapel of Golgotha in the southern one. To the east the new edifice was limited by the numerous small oratories erected in memory of certain events connected with the Passion.

The two major additions by the reconstructed sanctuary were a circular dome over the Holy Sepulcher itself on the west, and a church with a semicircular choir on the east. Of the two much subsists, in spite of repeated alterations and damages.

The Khwarazmian Tartars, a brutal people from the east of the Caspian, invaded Palestine in 1244 leaving a path of slaughtered Christians and Moslems and complete desolation wherever they set foot. They burned the Church of the Holy Sepulcher, but it was restored before the end of the century in a form not very dissimilar to the present. In 1400 two new domes were added, and in 1555 restorations were carried out by the Franciscans under the guidance of Boniface of Ragusa, Guardian of Mount Zion, who adhered closely to the twelfth century model.

In 1719 the church was partially rebuilt in order to make safe its many insecure parts. An accidental fire in 1808 left only a shell of it intact. The Greek Orthodox Church was now able to secure the principal rights to the buildings. With a firman from Constantinople authorizing the reconstruction of the gutted Basilica, it erected a new church in 1810. The Armenians joined in advancing necessary funds for this. Fifty years later France and Russia repaired the large dilapidated dome; but today the sanctuary is a sorrowful sight. Throughout the church, innumerable braces, placed by the British Government during the years 1935–1939, support the age-old structure and keep it from crumbling and crashing to the pavement.

The Atrium, or paved courtyard, in front of the church measures about eighty feet long and fifty-four feet wide and has vaulted chambers underneath. It is bounded on the south by the Greek Orthodox Convent of Gethsemane; on the east by the Greek Convent of Abraham—which occupies the west side of the Elia Forum—the Armenian Chapel of St. James, and the Coptic Chapel of the Archangel Michael; and on the northeast by the Greek Chapel of St. Mary the Egyptian, above which is the Roman Catholic Chapel of the Agony of the Virgin.

On the upper terrace of the Greek Convent of Abraham is found the small chapel of Abraham, where Anglican clerical visitors are permitted to celebrate Holy Communion by special permission of the Greek Orthodox Patriarch. The Chapel of St. Mary the Egyptian is scarcely twelve feet square and was built in memory of the conversion of Mary the Egyptian. The legend relates that Mary, who had led a gay life in Egypt, embarked from Alexandria for a pilgrimage to the Holy City. Upon her arrival at the Jerusalem gate, an angel forbade the sinful woman entrance. She retired to the desert to live a life of penance. Starving and in rags, she was discovered by a holy hermit. He instructed her in the truths of the Gospel and later, convinced of her sincere repentance and piety, gave her Holy Communion. Coming one day to visit his convert, the hermit found that she had died and was about to be buried by a God-fearing lion. He performed the last rites for Mary before lowering her into the lion-dug grave.

On the west of the Atrium are three Greek chapels: St. James, for the faithful of the Byzantine-Arab rite; Mary Magdalene; and the Forty Martyrs, with a massive bell tower. The tower was built about 1170 by the Crusaders and formerly stood apart from the chapel. The upper part has been destroyed; but it contained blind arches pierced by windows, and above these had an octagonal dome surrounded by pinnacles. Three column bases near the south end of the courtyard and one built into the wall can be observed today and are the remains of the twelfth century colonnade which stood here.

The south façade dates almost entirely from the time of the Crusaders. It is divided into an upper and a lower story. The lower has twin doors, the right of which has been closed from the time of Saladin. It is interesting to note, at this point, that the post of custodian of the church is hereditary in two Muhammedan families of Jerusalem. Since 1244 one family has kept the key, while the other has had the right of opening the door. Immediately inside the entrance of the sanctuary, on the left, is seen the divan of the caretakers. Every morning one of the four communities living within the Basilica—Greek Orthodox, Armenian, Copts, or Roman Catholic—pay for the opening of the door.

In the center of the Rotunda rises the notorious Chapel of the Holy Sepulcher, the Fourteenth Station of the Via Dolorosa. Of native rose-colored and white crystalline limestone with marble accessories, it was reconstructed in 1810 by the architect Commenos of Mitylene, whose name is recorded in an inscription just inside the inner doorway. It is twenty-six feet long and seventeen and a half feet wide, consisting of two chambers. The lateral walls are adorned with sixteen pillars and crowned by a balustrade of columns, surmounted by a little cupola in the Muscovite style. This curiously shaped, tent-roofed turret is hollow in the center and has windows for ventilation.

Outside the entrance to the chapel proper, which is a low, narrow door on the east, is what might be called a vestibule, consisting of two stone benches and large candelabra. The front is richly adorned with paintings and lamps. Entering, one comes into the Chapel of the Angel, in the center of which is a stone, inserted in a pedestal, said to be a fragment of the one which closed the door of the Tomb and was rolled away by the Angel. Fifteen lamps burn here, five belonging to the Greeks, five to the Catholics, four to the Armenians, and one to the Copts.

From the Chapel of the Angel one stoops to enter the Tomb proper, a room only six and a half feet long and six feet wide, so narrow that only three or four persons are permitted to kneel briefly before the Tomb at the same time. This Holy Sepulcher, seen on the right, is covered by a cracked marble slab, much worn by the lips of the pilgrims. It is five feet long, two feet wide, and three feet high. Mass is said daily at this altar. The Greeks celebrate their mass at one o'clock in the afternoon; the Armenians, at half past two; and the Roman Catholics at four. It is believed that below the marble covering, which is of early date, there is a rock-tomb, for in the time of the Crusaders the inner chamber of the Chapel of the Holy Sepulcher contained a niche-tomb. From the ceiling hang forty-three handsome lamps, fed with olive oil and kept constantly burning, four belonging to the Copts, and thirteen each to the Greeks, Catholics, and Armenians. In leaving the Chapel of the Tomb one walks backwards, always facing the Tomb for respect.

Under the single roof of the Church of the Holy Sepulcher are innumerable sites of veneration. Each sacred spot has tremendous importance to some sect of visiting pilgrims and is stamped with traditional significance and sincere belief. Therefore one must not be too skeptical of the rites performed continually in the massive edifice. Whether the modern pilgrim believes the legends behind these simple-hearted rites is of little importance. It is essential, however, to recognize the symbolism around which the legends grew and give sympathetic understanding to the naïve believers. One must realize that the present crowding together of so many holy sites, in so incongruous a manner, was not originated with any intention to deceive. Instead it, without doubt, grew out of services held in remote periods at different spots for the instruction of the simple pilgrims, very few of whom were able to read for themselves the words of the Gospels. Undoubtedly, in order to make the story more vivid and understandable, different sites or chapels were set apart for reading definite portions of the Scripture. Another point not to be overlooked is the dire necessity for having "progressive stations" in order physically to care for the ever-coming groups of pilgrims—pilgrims of many races and creeds. As time went on, the purely commemorative character of the church, chapel, or oratory probably began to be forgotten, and tradition began to mark exact locations with precise Biblical happenings; thus, around a perfectly innocent and even praiseworthy beginning grew misunderstandings, misrepresentations, and finally shameful abuses. One interested in the traditional customs of a race or creed must not be offended by grotesque, absurd, grossly idolatrous, and dishonoring Christian practices.

Among the revered sites in the Church of the Holy Sepulcher (listed in alphabetical order with no regard for their biblical sequence, their relative importance or religious significance, or their architectural beauty) are: the Chapel of Adam, which housed until 1808 the monuments of Godfrey of Bouillon and Baldwin I; the Chapel of the Agony of the Virgin; the Chapel of the Apparition; the Chapel of the Archangel Michael; the Chapel of Derision, or of the Crowning with Thorns; the Chapel of St. Helena, where once stood Constantine's Basilica called the Martyrion; the Chapel of the Invention of the Cross; the Chapel of St. Longinus, dedicated to the Roman soldier who with his spear pierced the side of Jesus; the Chapel of St. Mary Magdalene, by tradition the place where Jesus met Mary Magdalene after his resurrection; [25] the Chapel of the Mocking—that is, of the insults heaped upon Christ by the High Priests, the Scribes, the ancients of the Jews, and the rabble; the Chapel of the Nailing to the Cross, which contains the Tenth and Eleventh Stations on the Via Dolorosa—a Catholic chapel constructed where, according to tradition, Christ was disrobed and nailed to the Cross; the Chapel of the Parting of the Garments; the Chapel of the

[25] St. John 20:1–18.

Raising of the Cross, or the Twelfth Station of the Via Dolorosa; the Convent of the Franciscans who officiate in the Basilica; a Coptic Chapel, obtained in 1573 by the Copts for the celebration of their liturgy; the dwellings of church officials; the Franciscan Sacristy; the Office of the Greek Archimandrite, who is Guardian of the Church of the Holy Sepulcher; the Pillar of the Scourging; the Prison of Christ; the Rectangular Church; the Rotunda, or ancient Anastasis of Constantine; the Seven Arches of the Virgin—relics of the reconstruction carried out in the church in the eleventh century; the Stabat, which is the Thirteenth Station of the Cross; the Stone marking the site where the women stood afar off beholding the Crucifixion, and where the Virgin afterward stood and witnessed the anointments; the Stone of Unction; the Tombs of Nicodemus and Joseph of Arimathea; and the Tomb of Sir Philip D'Aubeny, an English Crusader who took part in the expedition of Frederick II in 1228.

THE TOMB OF ADAM

An ancient Greek legend places the tomb of Adam in the Church of the Holy Sepulcher. The legend relates that when Christ was crucified his blood ran down through the "rent made in the rock by the earthquake" and dropped on the skull of Adam, restoring our first ancestor to life. This has given rise to the custom, mainly practiced in the Greek Orthodox Church, of representing at the foot of the Crucified a skull and crossbones.

Just inside the doorway of the Chapel of Adam are two benches; one on either side. That on the left marks the spot where once stood the cenotaph of Duke Godfrey of Bouillon, the first Crusader ruler of Jerusalem. His tombstone disappeared at the time of the great fire of 1808. It is interesting to note that Godfrey was styled a duke because, in his humble piety, he declined the royal title, refusing to wear a kingly diadem in the city where his Saviour had worn a crown of thorns.

The tomb of his brother Baldwin, the first King, is marked by the bench on the right side of the doorway. Farther on in the chapel one is shown the tomb of Melchizedec, where, according to legend, the skull of Adam was buried.

THE CHAPEL OF ST. HELENA

The Armenian Chapel of St. Helena is a very picturesque structure, of which the northern and southern sides are partly rock, cased with masonry. The rough floor is sixteen feet below the level of the Sepulcher and is reached by a flight of twenty-nine stone steps. The chamber measures sixty-five feet long by forty-two feet wide.

In the seventh century a smaller sanctuary was erected by Modestus, from which the present substructures date. It is divided into a central nave with lateral aisles by four heavy antique Byzantine columns with dilapidated massive basket capitals patched with plaster. The monolithic columns used to shed tears, if we believe tradition. It contains two altars: one dedicated to St. Dismas, the penitent thief to whom Jesus made the promise, "Today you will be with me in Paradise"; and the other, to the Empress Helena. Close to the latter is shown the stone seat upon which Helena rested while superintending the excavations in search of Christ's Cross; but, unfortunately for the legend, history cannot prove that she did institute such a search. The tradition connecting her with the Invention of the Cross and the building with Constantine of the Church of the Holy Sepulcher did not originate until more than half a century after her time. Her contemporaries mention none of the circumstances related in the legend.

The church formerly belonged to the Abyssinians but was seized by the Armenians during the plague of 1838, when the Abyssinians in Jerusalem all perished.

Another interesting legend connected with this age-old site

informs us that originally an orifice here, now a plastered-up window, reached down into purgatory, and that upon entering this sanctuary one could distinctly hear the cries and screaming and groaning of anguished souls undergoing punishment.

THE CHAPEL OF ST. LONGINUS

The Chapel of St. Longinus does not seem to have been dedicated to him earlier than the sixteenth century. Longinus, the Roman soldier who pierced Christ's side, is said to have been blind in one eye which recovered its sight when touched by some of the "water and blood" which gushed from the wound. The tradition goes on to say that Longinus repented and became a Christian.

THE CHAPEL OF THE AGONY OF THE VIRGIN

One must look through a barred window into the Roman Catholic Chapel of the Agony of the Virgin, said to mark the spot where Mary stood during the Crucifixion. It contains a beautiful painted-glass window. Originally the chapel was a porch with a staircase leading up to its barred doorway. The question as to who had the right to sweep the staircase was the cause of a sanguinary encounter between the Catholic and Greek monks some years ago.

THE CHAPEL OF THE APPARITION

The Chapel of the Apparition dates from the fourteenth century and is the principal possession of the Catholics within the Church. Tradition relates that here Christ met his mother after the Resurrection, and the central altar is dedicated to her. Of this apparition the Gospel does not speak; but long-standing tradition has perpetuated its memory in the Church.

THE CHAPEL OF THE INVENTION
OF THE CROSS

A rough rock-hewn staircase in the southeastern corner of the Chapel of St. Helena descends thirteen steps to the Greek Chapel of the Invention of the Cross. The last three steps are of the original rock. The chapel, about twenty-four feet across and sixteen feet high, is a disused cistern where Helena discovered the three crosses, according to tradition. The true Cross was identified by the circumstance that when it was laid beside a dying woman it restored her to perfect health, the other two having failed to perform the miracle.

THE CHAPEL OF THE PARTING
OF THE GARMENTS

The Armenian Chapel of the Parting of the Garments dates from the twelfth century and was built in memory of the biblical passage in St. John 19:23–24, which relates: "When the soldiers had crucified Jesus they took his garments and made four parts, one for each soldier. But his tunic was without seam, woven from top to bottom; so they said one to another, 'Let us not tear it, but cast lots for it to see whose it shall be.' "

THE CHAPEL OF THE RAISING
OF THE CROSS

This chapel marks the traditional spot where the Cross was fastened in the rock and the places where the crosses of the two thieves stood. It was here that Jesus said, " 'It is finished'; and . . . bowed his head and gave up his spirit." The chapel marks the Twelfth Station of the Via Dolorosa.

THE FRANCISCAN SACRISTY

In this Franciscan chapel one sees the reputed sword and spurs of Godfrey of Bouillon, and a later Crusader's cross. These objects are used in creating Knights of the Order of the Holy Sepulcher.

THE PILLAR OF THE SCOURGING

The Pillar of the Scourging, formerly shown in the House of Caiaphas, was transferred to the Church of the Holy Sepulcher by the Crusaders. Pilgrims touch the pillar with a stick which is kept here, and then kiss the stick. Legend has it that this chapel stands on the site of the house of Joseph of Arimathea.

THE PRISON OF CHRIST

Since the twelfth century, this whitewashed Greek Orthodox chapel has been shown as the prison of Christ and the two thieves, where they were held during the preparation for the Crucifixion. At its entrance one finds "the stocks," two round holes in a marble slab.

THE RECTANGULAR CHURCH

According to tradition the Rectangular Church occupies the site of Joseph's garden. It contains the Greek Cathedral, called the Catholicon, and the Arch of the Emperor, a small stone chalicelike column with a rounded top, which, according to ancient fable, marks the Center of the Earth. Two Episcopal thrones are found on the north and south sides, the former designed for the Patriarch of Antioch and the latter for the Patriarch of Jerusalem.

THE STABAT

The Thirteenth Station of the Cross marks the alleged spot where Mary received the body of Jesus from the Cross. The

Catholics also hold this site sacred as the spot where Mary stood when Christ said, according to St. John 19:26–27, "Woman, behold your son!" and then to the disciple, "Behold your mother!"

THE STONE OF UNCTION

The Stone of Unction is today covered by a piece of polished red stone, placed almost on a level with the ground. Upon this rock, according to tradition, Joseph of Arimathea and Nicodemus laid the body of Jesus to be anointed and bound in a white linen cloth before burial in the tomb.

THE TOMBS OF NICODEMUS AND JOSEPH OF ARIMATHEA

Since the sixteenth century tradition has placed the Tombs of Nicodemus and Joseph, "a good and righteous man from the Jewish town of Arimathea," in two Jewish sepulchral chambers near the Tomb of Christ. Joseph, whose rock-hewn tomb was used for Jesus, is said to have made arrangements that when he and Nicodemus died their bodies should be laid in tombs close to Christ's and not in the empty tomb originally intended for himself, where Christ's body had lain for a time.

THE TOMB OF SIR PHILIP D'AUBENY

Sir Philip D'Aubeny was the tutor of King Henry III, who, crowned when only a child of eight years of age, was entrusted to his care during the protectorship of the able Earl of Pembroke. Before that, during the reign of King John, D'Aubeny was among the barons who signed the Magna Charta. He left England in 1222 for the holy wars in Palestine, where he resided for fourteen years, dying in 1236. The marble slab bearing his epitaph also displays a Norman shield with his armorial bearings.

GOLGOTHA AND THE GARDEN TOMB

So they took Jesus, and he went out, bearing his own cross.[26]

And when they came to the place which is called The Skull, there they crucified him.[27]

When it was evening, there came a rich man from Arimathea, named Joseph, who also was a disciple of Jesus. He went to Pilate and asked for the body of Jesus. Then Pilate ordered it to be given to him.[28]

Nicodemus . . . came bringing a mixture of myrrh and aloes, about a hundred pounds weight. They took the body of Jesus, and bound it in linen cloths with the spices, as is the burial custom of the Jews. Now in the place where he was crucified there was a garden, and in the garden a new tomb where no one had ever been laid. So because of the Jewish day of Preparation, as the tomb was close at hand, they laid Jesus there.[29]

———•———

A brisk five-minute walk almost due north down Nablus Road from Damascus Gate brings one to a narrow lane on the right. At the end of this blind alley is the entrance to the Garden Tomb. This garden, thought by some authorities to contain the Sepulcher of Christ, is a quiet, restful, inspiring spot, at the foot of a tomb-covered green hill, just outside the ancient walls of Jerusalem. The Sepulcher is a rock-tomb on the north side of the garden at the foot of a rocky knoll and contains three divisions or "mastabas." It is here that worshipers, especially Protestants, gather at sunrise on Easter for quiet contemplation and inspiration.

Since the year 1842, when Otto Thenius, a German scholar,

26 St. John 19:17.
27 St. Luke 23:33.
28 St. Matthew 27:57-58.
29 St. John 19:39-42.

first made the suggestion, many people, including General Gordon, the hero of Khartoum, have supposed that the knoll above Jeremiah's Grotto is the true site of Golgotha. This hill, just east of the garden, is commonly referred to today as Gordon's Calvary. It is interesting to note that the site, owned by the British Government, has no church. In the precipitous south cliff are some natural cavities which the famous soldier thought "bore a rough resemblance to the human form" and especially to a skull.

DAMASCUS GATE

As pilgrims on our way to Golgotha and the Garden Tomb, we hurried entirely too fast through Damascus Gate. It is important that we return to this significant landmark for a careful and more leisurely examination of its architectural and historical grandeur.

Damascus Gate is the most imposing of the present gates, and in all probability occupies the site of the northern gate at the time of Christ. This is indicated by the existence of two ancient tower chambers, one on either side, and the vestiges of a massive arched side gateway just inside the entrance. The remains consist of what all authorities agree in describing as ancient Roman masonry of the Herodian period.

The Arabic name for Damascus Gate is Bab el 'Amud, Gate of the Pillar. In the little Transjordanian town of Madeba one can see the ruins of a church of the fifth century, the floor of which is a unique mosaic map of Palestine and surrounding countries, showing the position of the churches at that period. The map shows a high pillar at this gate, which undoubtedly explains the name Gate of the Pillar.

Another name for it in Arabic is Bab en-Nasr, or Gate of Victory. Being the finest of the present portals, it is the one by which conquerors have usually entered. Above the gate on the city side an inscription records that Suleiman restored it in 1537.

GOOD FRIDAY

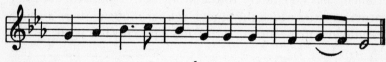

1

All centuries sing praises, O my Christ, praises for Thy burial.

2

Joseph of Arimathea gently took Thee down from the cross and laid Thee in his own new tomb.

3

Women brought ointments and sweet spices to Thee, O my Christ!

4

The women with their perfumes went early to the tomb.

5

Out of love for Him, Joseph and Nicodemus prepared Him for burial.

6

With bitter tears and aching heart, the Virgin cried.

7

O sweet Son, O Light of my eyes, how did they bury Thee!

8

Come, all creation, let us make lamentation for the Saviour!

9

Let us scatter precious perfume as did the women.

10

We praise Thy power, Thou who hast abolished death.

11

Give Thy people salvation, O God, and Peace to Thy church.

BY THY DEATH WE LIVE

1

O Christ, who Thy Father obeyedst,
And entrustedst Thyself to His keeping,
By Thy death Thou didst save the captives of sin.
With a garment of righteousness Thou didst clothe them.

2

Be near when grief overcomes me
And I walk amid clouds of thick darkness.
Send Thy peace and Thy light to show me the way,
That with confidence I may walk and not stumble.

3

When death overtakes me, dear Christ,
Turn my eyes to the cross, love revealing:
Comfort me with assurance of redemption
And let me enter Thy presence with great gladness.

FATHER, FORGIVE THEM

1

Dear Christ, we saw not Thee at all
When Thou wert on this earth;
We did not see the stable small
Wherein occurred Thy birth;
But we believe the stories dear
That prove Thou wert so very near.

2

The men that took Thy life away,
Dear Christ, we did not know;
"Father, forgive them," Thou didst pray,
"They know not what they do."
It is by faith the way we see
In which they feared to follow Thee.

3

And when they laid Thee in the tomb
We were not there to see;
And on that lovely Easter morn
We did not welcome Thee;
But we believe the open grave
Finished Thy plan the world to save.

IT IS FINISHED

1

"It is finished," said the Saviour
As He bowed His head and died.
Victory is now triumphant
And for all time shall abide.

2

Long ago the Christ was promised
As a prophet, priest, and king.
For this great and wondrous blessing
Grateful hearts to Him we bring.

3

But it grieves us when we realize
That our life should cause His death;
On the cruel cross He suffered,
So the sacred story saith.

4

But He lives again! We listen
To that voice that brings us peace;
Heaven and earth resound with echoes
That shall never, never cease.

THE LOVE OF GOD

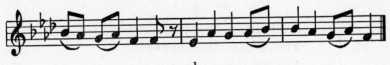

1

The world has a precious Friend—
No other can compare
With the steadfastness of His love.
No gift so great has ever been given.
Who of our earthly friends
Would offer such a sacrifice?
This Friend suffered and died for us.
His Love is beyond our understanding.

2

He was born in a lowly manger
Yet redeemed us with a Cross.
He ascended to heavenly heights.
And patiently hears our supplications.
Every human face should shine
With the glow of His light
Remembering always that
The world has a precious Friend.

O DEATH, WHERE IS THY VICTORY!

1

O Son of God whose power is o'er
The earth and heaven above,
None fear the darkness of the tomb,
Who live in faith and love.

Chorus

O Christ, Son of Mary,
The dead shall rise in Thee

2

They said, who saw the Holy One,
With malefactors slain,
"Thou life of all, and all of life,
Hast tasted death and pain!"

3

Since death has died upon the cross
And life to us is given,
We will not fear the judgment day
But rest in hope of heaven.

O MY BELOVED

1

I went at night to the garden, and with a heavy heart
I wept and prayed for comfort Thou only couldst impart.

Chorus

O Beloved, O Beloved, how deplorable Thy state!
Who has caused Thee thus to suffer, urged by cruelty and hate!

2

"O let this cup pass from me, if it can be Thy will!"
"My child, I'll share it with thee, so let thy heart be still."

3

Great was my grief and sorrow, my work was not yet done;
The multitudes were waiting—my work had just begun!

4

Upon the cross they nailed me, and mocked as they passed by,
No human hand relieved me, and I was left to die.

5

Behold, daughter of Zion, my weariness and pain.
Longing for human comfort, I watched all night in vain.

THE SUFFERING OF CHRIST

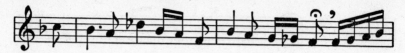

1

"They know not what they do—forgive them, Father!"
So prayed the Christ in agony and pain.
Their intercessor He: for them He suffered,
Yet, through it all, not once did He complain.

2

He tasted weariness, our dear Redeemer.
And all our sins He willingly forgave;
That people of all lands might be God's children.
Exceeding great His love—the world to save!

CHRIST AROSE

1

Christ has risen from the dead:
By death He conquered death,
Thus giving life to all who die.

GOOD TIDINGS TO THE FAITHFUL

1

To all, O Ye Faithful, good tidings have come!
Let us sing and be joyful—our Lord is arisen!

2

Today Christ is risen redeeming His people.
He rose to give life and salvation to all.

3

O happiest day, O day of rejoicing,
O day of salvation, when Jesus arose!

4

This is the day of our Lord's resurrection,
We should give thanks and bear witness for Him.

5

The cup that Christ drank, for our sakes, was how bitter.
Yes, death on the cross our redemption to gain!

6

Our Lord by His victory Paradise won,
He gave us the promise of sharing His joy.

7

An angel appeared, in the dawn, by the tomb
To tell the glad tidings: "Christ has arisen!"

8

To the women he said: "Fear not, but be joyful.
Your Lord lives again, and death is no more."

SAVE US, O SON OF MAN

Easter

1

Save us, O Son of man!
Thou who hast risen!
Let us praise Thee
Hallelu, Hallelu!

2

Save us, O Son of man!
On this Easter morn
We praise Thee
Hallelu, Hallelu!

CHAPTER X

The Pilgrimage to Jericho and the River Jordan

JERICHO (Er-Riha in Arabic) is approximately twenty-one miles to the east-northeast of Jerusalem and five miles west of the river Jordan. It lies in the west part of the fertile flat belt which stretches to the east and west of the Jordan, commonly called the Jordan valley. The Arabs call this valley El Ghor, the Valley. The short pilgrimage from Jerusalem to Jericho and the river is a unique and delightful journey for the Holy Land pilgrim. The ever winding ancient road, which descends 3,392 feet in its downward sweep from the Holy City to the river, is rich in scenery and biblical and historical association. Its geological formation is unparalleled.

Leaving the city, the road passes Gethsemane, ascends the west slope of Olivet, swings to the east past the valley of the fig-tree which Christ cursed when he found it fruitless,[1] to the small Moslem village of Bethany. Here one finds the Tomb of Lazarus, the Castle of Lazarus (commonly thought to be the House of Simon the Leper) and the House of Martha and Mary.

The Castle of Lazarus is approximately twenty-five yards to the southwest of the Tomb and is a tall ruin. Its lower part is of

[1] Refer to St. Matthew 21:17-22.

large drafted blocks of an unknown date, but the upper part of the tower was built by Millicent, the wife of Fulk, third Crusader King of Jerusalem, to protect the nunnery that she established here in 1134 on the site of a large fourth century monastery, next to the remains of a fourth century Church of St. Lazarus. She erected the nunnery primarily for her sister Yvette, who served it as abbess from 1157 to 1178. After the conquest of the Arabs this sanctuary was neglected, and the dilapidated structure today offers pilgrims a mere reflection of its one-time splendor.

The House of Martha and Mary, sisters of Lazarus and disciples of Jesus, is about a thousand feet east of the Castle of Lazarus. Some claim that here are the authentic remains of Millicent's nunnery. There is considerable diversity in the traditions regarding the houses of Martha, Mary, and Lazarus and Simon the Leper. Having been neglected since the Arab conquest this sanctuary stands in complete ruins today.

From the village of Bethany, one returns to the historical Jericho Road over which Christ must have traveled several times on the way to and from Jerusalem, Jericho, and the Jordan. The present road follows the ancient route from the Jordan valley, which was the boundary between the Tribes of Judah and Benjamin, and which the Jews from northern and eastern tribes followed when they came to sacrifice in the Temple.

The steep descent into the Wady el Hod must soon be begun, passing an old khan and the Apostles' Fountain. Arabs call the fountain Hod el 'Azariyeh; but the fifteenth century Christians gave it the name Apostles' Fountain, and the Apostles must have refreshed themselves many times at this spring, the only one between Bethany and the Jordan valley. It is also identified with the "waters of En Shemesh," [2] one of the places mentioned in the boundary line between Judah and Benjamin.

The road continues in the Wady el Hod, with bare and rounded rock hills on either side, passing the Russian Khan el

[2] Joshua 15:7.

Ahmar. Excavations in 1928 brought to light the plan of St. Euthymius' monastery and church founded about 428. The crypt in which the tomb of the founder was perhaps buried was also discovered.

Halfway between Jerusalem and Jericho the Khan Hathrur, better known as the Good Samaritan's Inn, is passed. Tradition has long identified this dismally lonely spot as the scene of Christ's parable of the man who fell among thieves. The next descent is 'Akabet ej Jerad, Ascent of the Locusts, and then we pass the new road which branches off to the right, constructed for the convenience of the Muhammedan pilgrims who annually visit En Neby Mousa, the reputed tomb of Moses.

Continuing our journey on the old Roman road, we soon come to Wady el Kelt, a very deep gorge on the left, between walls of gigantic rocks.

Wady el Kelt, the continuation of the Wady Fara, northeast of Jerusalem, is a picturesque, wild gorge with the largest stream of water in this part of the Holy Land. The stream furnishes the power for a turbine engine and mill near the waterfall. An aqueduct, a restoration of an ancient one, conducts water down to the Jordan plain.

This valley has been thought to correspond to the brook Cherith, where Elijah was fed by the ravens.[3] It has also been identified with the Valley of Achor, where Joshua caused Achan to be stoned for the sin he had committed in stealing articles from the fallen Jericho.[4]

On the other side of Wady el Kelt, the precipitous gorge, are the remains of an ancient Crusader aqueduct and a small waterfall which, according to tradition, was the setting for the Twenty-third Psalm.

On the north side of the valley stands the imposing Greek Monastery of St. George, built in a large cavern in the rocky face of the cliff on the site and substructures of the ancient mon-

[3] I Kings 17:3-5.
[4] Joshua 7:1-26.

astery of Khozeba of Justinian's time—of which there are a few mosaics and other remains still in evidence. In an important pass on the only watercourse in this section of Palestine, the convent suffered from the endless stream of Palestinian invaders. According to Roman Catholic tradition, it was here that St. Joachim had hid himself to bewail the sterility of his betrothed, Anna, when in a vision the angel announced to him the birth of the Virgin.

A little farther on, on the left, is the upper of the two castles called Beit Jabr el Fokani and et Tahtani, the Upper and Lower Houses of Jabr. Archaeologists have suggested that these ruins may occupy the sites of the castles of Thrax and Tauros which in ancient times guarded the pass.

Proceeding, we soon reach the steep and rocky descent called 'Akabet ej Jabr (Ascent of the Jabr), which forms the last part of the road before the plain. The view from the hill is breathtaking. The whole Jordan plain spreads before the pilgrim with a backdrop of the ever-blue Hills of Moab. Jericho lies like an oasis in the midst of the flat plain. Kasr Hajlah—the ancient Beth Hogla, now a Greek Orthodox monastery—appears in the desert a refuge between Jericho and the Dead Sea.

On emerging into the plain we cross Tell Abul'-'alaik (Hill of the Leeches), which marks the site of the Herodian Jericho. Opposite this, on the right of the road, are the remains of an ancient pool called Birket Mousa (Pool of Moses), also constructed by Herod the Great. It is 188 yards long by 157 yards wide and was part of a great system of irrigation which once made a green paradise. The Roman Catholics suggest that it was here that Herod had his brother-in-law, the nineteen-year-old high priest Aristobulus, drowned in order to rid himself of the last of the Hasmoneans.

The road crosses the plain to Jericho, "the city of palm trees." [5] Here pilgrims never fail to visit near-by Elisha's Fountain and

5 Deuteronomy 34:3 and II Chronicles 28:15.

the Mount of Temptation, where tradition places Christ's forty-day sojourn in the wilderness. Elisha's Fountain ('Ain es Sultan, Spring of the Sultan) is two miles northwest of Jericho on the road, flanked with banana and orange groves, leading either to Nablus through the Wady el Fara or straight to Tiberias through the village of Beisan. It is still a good and copious spring, its source concealed in the bottom of a large masonry millpond. Early tradition identified it with that which Elisha "healed"; hence its Christian name. The Byzantines constructed a church here in honor of Elias, but no portion of the structure remains today.

From Jericho, the village of mud huts, a new road can be taken along the north side of Wady el Kelt to the traditional site of Christ's baptism by John the Baptist in the river Jordan.[6] Along the way to this famous site of annual pilgrimage two historical sites, Khirbet Teleilat and the Greek Monastery of St. John, make noteworthy pauses.

Khirbet Teleilat, thought to be the site of Gilgal "in the east border of Jericho," where the Israelites pitched their first camp after the passage through the Jordan, is just off the main road on the return to Jericho from the river. It was here, according to tradition, that the twelve stones collected from the bed of the river were erected as a memorial to future generations, "that all the people of the earth might know the hand of the Lord, that it is mighty." [7] At Gilgal the Israelites readopted the rite of circumcision, and "the reproach of Egypt" was "rolled off" from them.[8] The cunning Gibeonites came here to make a league with Joshua.[9] Gilgal was one of the seats of the Judges in the time of Samuel.[10] Here "Samuel hewed Agag in pieces before the

---

6 St. Matthew 3:13–17, St. Mark 1:9–11, and St. Luke 3:21–22.
7 Joshua 4:19–24.
8 Joshua 5:7–9.
9 Joshua 9:6.
10 I Samuel 7:15–16.

Lord." [11] Elisha cast meal into the pot at Gilgal, where "there was a dearth in the land," and made the deadly pottage safe for consumption.[12] Here the "captain of the host of the Lord" appeared before Joshua and bade him go forward and conquer Jericho.[13]

Seen here today are a few ruins of an ancient pool, a few large tamarisks, and a small mound known as Tell Jeljul. To the south can be seen the Birket el Jeljulie with remains of ancient constructions and mosaic cubes scattered about.

The Greek Orthodox Monastery of St. John is called Deir Mar Yuhanna in Arabic, and Prodromos (Precursor) by the Greeks. This sanctuary was erected in memory of "John the son of Zechariah" who "went into all the region about the Jordan, preaching a baptism of repentance for the forgiveness of sin." [14] The church was in existence as early as the fourth century, for it is said that St. Mary of Egypt stopped at the monastery in 373. It was undoubtedly standing at the time of Justinian, and tradition asserts that St. Helena erected a church here over the cave in which John the Baptist dwelt. An earthquake in 1034 caused considerable damage, but it was restored by the Emperor Manuel Comnenus in the twelfth century. A further restoration was made by the Greeks in 1882, but an earthquake in 1927 again damaged the church and part of the convent. Some of the remains of the early construction can still be seen, however.

[11] I Samuel 15:33.
[12] II Kings 4:38–41.
[13] Joshua 5:13–14, 6:2.
[14] St. Luke 3:2–3.

BETHANY

And leaving them, he went out of the city to Bethany and lodged there.[15]

Bethany was near Jerusalem, about two miles off . . ,[16]

Now when Jesus was at Bethany in the house of Simon the leper, a woman came up to him with an alabaster jar of very expensive ointment, and she poured it on his head, as he sat at table.[17]

[Jesus said] ". . . she has done a beautiful thing to me . . . In pouring this ointment on my body she has done it to prepare me for burial. Truly, I say to you, wherever this gospel is preached in the whole world, what this woman has done will be told in memory of her." [18]

————•—•————

Bethany (called El 'Azariyeh, Place of Lazarus, by the Arabs) is today a poor Moslem hamlet with a mere 515 inhabitants. On the southeast slopes of Olivet, it consists of a confused collection of houses, built chiefly of stones taken from early Christian build-

[15] St. Matthew 21:17.
[16] St. John 11:18.
[17] St. Matthew 26:6–7.
[18] St. Matthew 26:10, 12–13.

ings. In this village Christ spent many hours with his friends
Lazarus, Mary and Martha.[19] In this village Christ "cried with a
loud voice, 'Lazarus, come out,'" and the dead Lazarus "came
out," having been restored to life.[20] Here "Mary took a pound of
costly ointment of pure nard and anointed the feet of Jesus and
wiped his feet with her hair," six days before the Passover.[21]

Bethany was adorned with churches and monasteries as early
as the fourth century. The Roman Paula, in the beginning of the
fifth century, visited a church constructed over the Tomb of
Lazarus. Millicent established a nunnery here in 1134. The sanctuaries fell to ruins after the Arab invasion, and toward the end
of the fourteenth century the Moslems transformed the ruins of
the church into a mosque. The crypt of St. Lazarus, also held in
reverence by Muhammedans, became inaccessible for Christians.

REJOICE BETHANY

(A Christian Chant)

1

Rejoice, O Bethany, for to thee the Christ is coming!
The dead He maketh to live, the Lord is He and none other.

2

Weeping and sad of heart, Martha welcomed the Master,
Told Him all her grief, and unburdened all her sorrow.

3

"Jesus, my Lord," she cried; "best of our friends and the dearest,
Help, for my heart is breaking over the death of my brother."

[19] St. Luke 10:38 and St. John 12:1–2.
[20] St. John 11:43–44. For the complete biblical reference read St. John 11:1–44.
[21] St. John 12:3. For other biblical references read St. Matthew 26:6–12, St. Mark
14:3–9, and St. John 12:2–3.

4

Tenderly answered the Christ: "Cease, dear friend, from thy
    weeping;
Again thy brother shall live, if Thou hast faith to believe it."

5

Then to the tomb they led Him, He the Lord and Redeemer;
"Lazarus, friend of my heart, quickly arise from thy slumber!"

6

Haste, O Martha and Mary, see this wonder of wonders!
Lazarus lives again! Give thanks to your Friend who is mighty!

7

Jesus, Lord of the world, Thee we reverently worship,
Though we were dead in our sins, life is now ours by Thy mercy!

THE TOMB OF LAZARUS

Now a certain man was ill, Lazarus of Bethany, the village of Mary
and her sister Martha.[22]

So the sisters sent to him, saying, "Lord, he whom you loved is ill." [23]

Now when Jesus came, he found that Lazarus had already been in
the tomb four days.[24]

When Martha heard that Jesus was coming, she went and met him
. . . [and said] "Lord, if you had been here, my brother would not
have died. And even now I know that whatever you ask from God,
God will give you." Jesus said to her, "Your brother will rise again." [25]

Then Jesus, deeply moved . . . , came to the tomb; it was a cave,
and a stone lay upon it. Jesus said, "Take away the stone." [26]

[22] St. John 11:1.
[23] St. John 11:3.
[24] St. John 11:17.
[25] St. John 11:20–23.
[26] St. John 11:38–39.

So they took away the stone. And Jesus . . . cried with a loud voice, "Lazarus, come out." The dead man came out, his hands and feet bound with bandages, and his face wrapped with a cloth. Jesus said to them, "Unbind him, and let him go." [27]

———•◆•———

Toward the end of the fourth century a church was built over the tomb of Lazarus. The authenticity of this sanctuary is supported by an uninterrupted series of documents from early Christian times to the arrival of the Crusaders. At the beginning of the twelfth century the church was given to the Canons of the Holy Sepulcher. In 1138 they renounced all rights that they held over the church in favor of the Benedictines of St. Anne. The church was unattended after the Arab conquest until toward the end of the fourteenth century, when the Muhammedans transformed its ruins into a mosque.

After the east entrance to the church was closed by the Moslems to all Christians, permission was purchased by Angelo of Messina, Father Custodian of the Holy Land, to open a new entrance on the north for Christian pilgrims. With candle or lamp one descends twenty-two well worn steps into a cavern containing the tomb. At the bottom of the cave is a small vestibule. A narrow opening in the wall, through which one can descend three more steps, leads into the mortuary chamber where, according to tradition, Lazarus was laid.[28]

LAZARUS' CHANT

[27] St. John 11:41, 43–44.
[28] For the complete biblical reference read St. John 11:1–44.

(*Singing*)

The birds from gladness sing
The happy time has come!
And may this joyful feast
Forever come and go!

(*Chanting*)

Ye people of the Christ
Today we may rejoice!
Good news to us is given
Of gladness and of light.

(*Shouting*)

Give us an egg unbroken
Else we the chimney break!

THE GOOD SAMARITAN'S INN

A man was going down from Jerusalem to Jericho, and he fell among robbers, who stripped him and beat him, and departed, leaving him half-dead. Now by chance . . . a Samaritan, as he journeyed, came to where he was; and when he saw him, he had compassion, and went to him and bound up his wounds, pouring on oil and wine; then he set him on his own beast and brought him to an inn, and took care of him.[29]

Khan Hathrur (Good Samaritan's Inn), above which stand the ruins of an old Crusader castle, is a rest house rebuilt in the last century. It is also known as Khan el Ahmar, the Red Inn, because of the red rock and soil in the vicinity. On the knoll where it stands there has been a caravanserai for centuries, a fortress for the protection of travelers against highwaymen. In its court are yet to be seen sections of stone walls and large fragments of mosaic pavements of fine design which are at least as old as the twelfth century.

[29] St. Luke 10:30-31, 33-34.

The road on both sides of the Khan is called Tala'at ed Dum, Ascent of the Blood, and corresponds to the "going up to Adummim." [30] According to St. Jerome, the Greek Orthodox Church called it "Red Mountain," and St. Jerome noted the general opinion in that church that the name had its origin in "the blood which was so often shed there by robbers."

JERICHO

And Moses went up from the plains of Moab unto the mountain of Nebo, to the top of Pisgah, that is over against Jericho. And the Lord shewed him . . . the plain of the valley of Jericho, the city of palm trees.[31]

And the Lord said unto Joshua, "See, I have given into thine hand Jericho." [32]

So the people shouted when the priests blew with the trumpets: and it came to pass, when the people heard the sound of the trumpet, and the people shouted with a great shout, that the wall fell down flat, so that the people went up into the city, every man straight before him, and they took the city.[33]

. . . and as he was leaving Jericho with his disciples and a great multitude, Bartimaeus, a blind beggar, the son of Timaeus, was sitting by the roadside. . . . "Son of David, have mercy on me!" . . . And Jesus said to him, "What do you want me to do for you?" And the blind man said to him, "Master, let me receive my sight." And Jesus said to him, "Go your way, your faith has made you well." And immediately he received his sight and followed him on the way.[34]

———•◦•———

[30] Joshua 15:7.
[31] Deuteronomy 34:1, 3.
[32] Joshua 6:2.
[33] Joshua 6:20. For the complete biblical reference see Joshua 6:1–27.
[34] St. Mark 10:46, 48, 51–52. For the complete biblical reference see St. Mark 10:46–52. Other references may be found in St. Matthew 20:29–34 and St. Luke 18:35–43.

Jericho of the Old Testament was north of the present village and near Elisha's Fountain ('Ain es Sultan). During the years 1907–1909 the German Oriental Society made extensive excavations on the hills west of Elisha's Fountain and definitely established the site of ancient Jericho. The entire course of the city was traced, the walls having been composed of sun-dried bricks on a foundation of unhewn stones. These are believed to be the remains of the Canaanitish walls which fell at the time of the Israelite invasion. Remains of a later wall, containing very large squared stones, are undoubtedly the foundations of the wall of Hiel the Bethelite. Many tiny house walls reveal that the dwellings were extremely small; numerous flint implements show that the metallurgy was not far advanced. Stone door sockets and mortars and much pottery also were exhumed.

At the time of Exodus, Jericho was a Canaanitish town of some importance. It was to this ancient city that Joshua and the Israelites first came after crossing the miraculously divided waters of the Jordan.[35] Around its walls "the people shouted" and "the priest blew" with the rams' horns and "the wall fell down flat so that the people went up into the city" and took it.[36] Joshua laid a curse at this time upon the man who should rebuild the city, saying, "Cursed be the man before the Lord, that riseth up and buildeth this city Jericho: he shall lay the foundation thereof in his firstborn, and in his youngest son shall he set up the gates of it." [37] This curse was fulfilled in the days of Ahab when Hiel the Bethelite rebuilt Jericho. "He laid the foundation thereof in Abiram his firstborn, and set up the gates thereof in his youngest son Segub, according to the word of the Lord, which he spake by Joshua the son of Nun." [38] The city later attained a certain degree of importance under the kings of Israel, became the center of a flourishing school of prophets, and was visited by Elijah and Elisha just before Elijah "went up by a whirlwind into

35 Joshua 3:13–17.
36 Joshua 6:12–20.
37 Joshua 6:26.
38 I Kings 16:34.

heaven" in a "chariot of fire." [39] After having witnessed Elijah's ascension, Elisha returned across the Jordan, miraculously divided by his command,[40] to Jericho. The "men of the city" complained that the water was "naught, and the ground barren"; whereupon he cast salt into the water and exclaimed, "I have healed these waters; there shall not be from thence any more death or barren land." [41]

Jericho reached its highest degree of prosperity and importance after Cleopatra, presented with the district by Mark Antony, sold it to Herod the Great. The city was then beautified with palaces, a hippodrome and amphitheater, and the castle of Cypros; and the surrounding plain was systematically irrigated to make magnificent gardens for the winter residence of the monarch. Herod died here in 4 B.C. but, in compliance with his instructions, was buried at Herodium, south of Bethlehem.

Christ visited the city several times, on one occasion healing the blind beggar Bartimaeus; on another occasion Zacchaeus, the wealthy tax collector, was completely transformed by his visit.[42] Soon after, Christ disclosed his Parable of the Pounds.[43]

In A.D. 325 Jericho became the seat of a bishopric. Many monks settled here to lead a solitary life under the guidance of St. Euthymius and St. Sabas. Justinian restored the Church of the Mother of God, and founded a large hospice for pilgrims here in the sixth century. The Medeba map represents Jericho as having many palm trees.

After the devastation of the hordes of Chosroes in 614, Jericho began to decline; and it was a mere heap of rubble by the twelfth century. The Crusaders revived the city and called it New Jericho, selecting the present site, slightly east of the two earlier cities, and fortifying it with a castle. A Church of the Holy Trinity also was erected. The new prosperity ended with the fall of

---

[39] II Kings 2:11. For the complete biblical reference read II Kings 2:1–11.
[40] II Kings 2:12–14.
[41] II Kings 2:19–22.
[42] St. Luke 19:1–10.
[43] St. Luke 19:11–27.

the Crusader kingdom and the disruption of the irrigation system upon which the fertility of the entire valley depended. The environs soon became a desert, and by the sixteenth century Jericho was no longer a center of great population. Under the Ottoman rule, however, it was made the headquarters of a mudir who administered a part of the Crown domains of the Jordan valley, extending from the Dead Sea to Tiberias. The British took the village from the Turks on February 21, 1918.

Today the tiny village of Jericho consists of a collection of flat-roofed mud huts with a few modern buildings. The native population of approximately four hundred is principally of a degenerated race of black Bedouins called Hawarneh, that is, inhabitants of the valley. Few Europeans reside here, except in the winter months. The altitude is 792 feet below sea level, and the climate and vegetation are subtropical. The exceedingly fertile soil of the valley produces flourishing gardens, and its fruits are famous. The Jericho orange is highly prized and is acclaimed as most delicious. The banana is profitably cultivated. The date palm, *Phoenix dactylifera* L., grows wild, especially on the eastern shores of the Dead Sea, and its fruit is much sought after.

The sycamore fig, the tree that Zacchaeus climbed to see Christ pass by,[44] is still prevalent as are two species of the zizyphus, a very thorny genus called by the natives *Sidr,* of which, according to tradition, Christ's crown of thorns was made. It is widely used by the nationals today for hedges. Sugar cane is widely cultivated, as it was in the time of the Crusaders if the ruined mills near 'Ain es Sultan are properly identified as sugar mills.

The Greek Orthodox Church maintains a church in Jericho, and the Russian Orthodox Church has an interesting hospice in the compound of which are the remains of a fourth century church with a mosaic pavement. The Franciscan Sisters operate a primary school in the village. During the fifteenth century the House of Zacchaeus began to be "located" and today it can be seen in the southeastern part of the village as a ruined tower-

[44] St. Luke 19:4.

like construction, most likely a mere portion of a small Crusader fort.

MOUNT OF TEMPTATION

And Jesus, full of the Holy Spirit, returned from the Jordan, and was led by the spirit for forty days in the wilderness, tempted by the devil.[45]

And the devil took him up, and showed him all the kingdoms of the world in a moment of time.[46]

———•——

A footpath can be followed about halfway up the steep hill traditionally known as the Mount of Temptation, past a number of Greek hermitages, to a Greek Orthodox monastery built around the traditional cave in which Christ "fasted forty days and forty nights." [47] The monastery is constructed directly in front of the cave and extends out over the footpath and even beyond the rugged cliff-side. While yet in the distance on the picturesque climb upward, it appears to hang from the cliffs—bulging, as it were, from the mouth of a cave. The balconies extend like eagle nests on forbidden summits.

A pilgrim does not fail to see the monastery, because there is no way to continue without banging on the heavy iron door for admittance and passage through the building to the opposite end, which opens upon the interrupted pathway. In 1902 the Greeks reconstructed the ancient chapel in front of the legendary grotto; and its glittering newness hardly blends with its antique surroundings. The ruins of the Chapel of the Temptation can also be observed.

In 1112 the Crusaders accepted this site as the authentic dwelling place of Christ immediately after he was baptized in the Jordan by John. Although there is no authoritative ground for

45 St. Luke 4:1–2. For the complete biblical references see St. Matthew 4:1–11, St. Mark 1:12–13, and St. Luke 4:1–12.

46 St. Luke 4:5.

47 St. Matthew 4:2.

the belief that the hill is the exact place where "the Spirit immediately drove him out into the wilderness," it meets all the physical requirements of the biblical recording, and has been accepted as such by countless pilgrims since Crusader times.

As one leaves the Greek monastery for the final climb to the summit, the phrase in St. Luke 4:5 comes to mind: "And the devil, taking him up into a high mountain"! [48] Truly it is "up," for the climb is hard for plainsmen. The view from the summit, however, which is 1,130 feet above the Jericho plain, surely fulfills the Scripture, "And the devil took him up, and showed him all the kingdoms of the world in a moment of time." [49] One sees the Mount of Olives, beside Jerusalem the Holy, topped with its famous Russian Orthodox bell tower; the Dead Sea; the beautiful blue hills of Moab; the breath-taking valley of the Jordan, with the tiny hamlet of mud huts called Jericho; and far into the land across the Jordan. The region across the Jordan is the ancient Gilead, now called the Balka. It is inhabited by different tribes of Bedouins, called the Balkawiyeh. The political name of the territory east of the Jordan is Transjordan.

Besides the magnificent view, one finds the remains of a Greek chapel and some Frankish ruins. A wall, surrounding the property of the Greeks, stands as if on guard over the entire mountain peak and remains an isolated fortress in the wilderness, protecting the traditional site where Christ stood to view "all the kingdoms of the world." The wildness and seclusion of this summit early attracted anchorites, among whom, it is said, was St. Chariton, in the beginning of the fifth century.

JORDAN RIVER

And Elisha sent a messenger unto him, saying, Go and wash in Jordan seven times, and thy flesh shall come again to thee, and thou shalt be clean. [50]

[48] Also St. Matthew 4:8.
[49] Revised Standard Version, St. Luke 4:5.
[50] II Kings 5:10.

And when they came to Jordan, they cut down wood.[51]

If thou hast run with the footmen, and they have wearied thee, then how canst thou contend with horses? and if in the land of peace, wherein thou trustedst, they wearied thee, then how wilt thou do in the swelling of Jordan? [52]

———•—•———

The Jordan (El Urdun, or Esh Sheri'a el Kebria, in Arabic) is a swift and tortuous stream, flowing for its entire course through a fertile alluvial valley. Its chief sources are at Benias in the Anti-Lebanon and the Hasbani springs between the Lebanons. There is a fall of three thousand feet between its source and the Dead Sea, its final resting place. From the Lebanon springs it flows across the Syrian border into Palestine and at seven feet above sea level passes into Lake Huleh, the Waters of Merom.[53]

The river then wends its way downward into the Sea of Galilee. In the twelve-mile run from Lake Huleh it drops 689 feet, the Sea of Galilee being 682 feet below sea level. From it to the Dead Sea is sixty-six miles as a crow flies, but the windings of the Jordan make approximately three times that distance, dropping another 610 feet and pouring 5,000,000 tons of water into the Dead Sea daily.

The muddiness of the water is caused by the swift undercurrent which stirs the loose soil along the banks and churns the river bed. The broad mouth is divided into two parts by a deposit of silt, and on this ever growing little island flamingoes are often to be observed.

The river has an average width of one hundred feet and an average depth of ten feet. It teems with various kinds of fish, and the thicket along its course, formed of willows, acacias, tamarisks, poplars, and countless shrubs and vines, abounds in bird and animal life—among which is the wild boar.

[51] II Kings 6:4.
[52] Jeremiah 12:5.
[53] Joshua 11:5-7.

THE PLACE OF BAPTISM

And Joshua rose early in the morning; . . . and came to Jordan, he and all the children of Israel, and lodged there before they passed over. And it came to pass, when the people removed from their tents, to pass over Jordan, . . . that the waters which came down from above stood and rose up upon an heap . . . and those that came down toward the sea of the plain, even the salt sea, failed, and were cut off: and the people passed over right against Jericho.[54]

And Elijah said unto him, "Elisha, tarry here, I pray thee; for the Lord hath sent me to Jericho." And he said, "As the Lord liveth, and as thy soul liveth, I will not leave thee." So they came to Jericho. . . . And they two went on . . . and they two stood by Jordan. . . . And Elijah took his mantle, and wrapped it together, and smote the waters, and they were divided hither and thither, so that they two went over on dry ground.[55]

[Elisha] took up . . . the mantle of Elijah . . . and went back, and stood by the bank of Jordan; and he took the mantle of Elijah . . . and smote the waters, and . . . they parted hither and thither: and Elisha went over.[56]

———————

To reach the Place of Christ's Baptism in the Jordan, which the Palestinians call Mahadet Hajlah or El Maghtas (the Place of Immersion), one must travel across the uncultivated salty plain west of Jericho to Kasr el Hajlah, the Greek Monastery of St. Gerassimos. Kasr el Hajlah is built on the foundations of an ancient monastery and displays some beautiful frescoes and mosaics estimated by archaeologists to be between seven and eight hundred years old. It is the ancient Beth Holgal, mentioned in the delimitation of the territories of Judah and Benjamin,[57] and is noted on the fifth century Medeba map.

The pilgrimage continues past the tepid spring of 'Ain el

[54] Joshua 3:1, 14, 16.
[55] II Kings 2:4, 6, 7, 8.
[56] II Kings 2:13, 14.
[57] Joshua 15:6.

Hajlah, around which the Greek monks have planted beautiful gardens and date palms. The prolific growth here is a proof of the fertility of the whole plain when irrigated. Then on to the road just beyond, built between chalk formations covered with gypsum and encrusted with salt. The vegetation in this area is very interesting and most peculiar. One common plant is a low chenopod from which alkali is made, the *Salsola Kali* L. A common spring flower is the brilliant pink bloom, consisting of a large cluster of small blossoms, of the bush *Statice pruinosa* L.

Descending into the lower-lying belt along the river, which is often submerged and always overgrown with thick vegetation, one soon comes to the Place of Immersion, an important ford.

Conveniently for the pilgrim, tradition has placed many biblical happenings at this ford. It is thought that, in this vicinity, the Israelites crossed the divided waters on "dry ground," while the "priests that bare the ark of the covenant of the Lord stood firm on dry ground in the midst of Jordan." [58]

"Out of the midst of Jordan . . . where the priests' feet stood firm," Joshua commanded "twelve men out of the people, out of every tribe a man," to gather every man "a stone upon his shoulder" and carry it over to Gilgal and erect a monument "for a memorial unto the children of Israel." Here also is the reputed place where both Elijah and Elisha smote the waters and divided them for an undisturbed passage. [59]

Naaman, "captain of the host of the king of Syria" and a great and honorable man, "mighty in valour," was washed clean of his leprosy in the waters of the Jordan, [60] while at this traditional site Elisha caused an iron axhead to swim. [61] The legend of St. Christopher, who carried the Christ child across the river, is likewise connected with this ford.

Legend has it that John, who "wore a garment of camel's hair,

[58] Joshua 3:17. For the complete biblical reference read the entire chapter.
[59] II Kings 2:8, 14.
[60] II Kings 5:1–14.
[61] II Kings 6:6.

and a leather girdle around his waist" and lived on locusts and wild honey, baptized here the hordes from Jerusalem and all Judea who came "confessing their sins." [62] The Baptist pronounced:

I baptize you with water for repentance, but he who is coming after me is mightier than I, whose sandals I am not worthy to carry; he will baptize you with the Holy Spirit and with fire. His winnowing fork is in his hand, and he will clear his threshing floor and gather his wheat into the granary, but the chaff he will burn with unquenchable fire.[63]

To make the spot even more sacred, ancient Bethabara has been traditionally placed here. To this river bank Jesus, "from Nazareth of Galilee," came "and was baptized by John in the Jordan."

And when he came up out of the water, immediately he saw the heavens opened and the Spirit descending upon him like a dove; and a voice came from heaven, "Thou art my beloved Son; with thee I am well pleased." [64]

Here annually come thousands of pilgrims, especially at the special ceremony on the day of Epiphany.

The Transjordanian bank, near the Baptismal, is also spotted with sacred sites. Not far away can be seen the remains of a Byzantine church, supposedly built by Emperor Anastasius in A.D. 500. Vestiges of a chapel, said to have been built in honor of St. Mary of Egypt, are also found here. Less than a mile away is Jebel Mar Elias, identified with the place opposite Jericho to the east of the Jordan from whence "Elijah went up by a whirlwind into heaven." [65]

[62] St. Matthew 3:4.

[63] St. Matthew 3:11-12. For further and complete references see St. Matthew 3:1-13, St. Mark 1:1-8, and St. Luke 3:1-17.

[64] St. Mark 1:10-11. For further and complete references see St. Matthew 3:13-17, St. Mark 1:9-11, and St. Luke 3:21-22.

[65] II Kings 2:11.

CHAPTER XI

Christian Folk Songs in the Holy Land

THE Arabian religious folk music included in this chapter and this study is recorded exactly as the writer heard it sung in some part of the Holy Land, without any attempt to include variants. It should be clearly understood that the music of the entire Near East is interconnected. Variants of the same folk song are found far outside the Holy Land. This study aims to present accurately recorded religious folk songs, notated as sung in such biblical centers as Jerusalem, Bethlehem, Jaffa, Ram Allah, Jericho, and Nazareth. The folk melodies and words are definitely local variants.

No attempt is made here to make the melodies and rhythm more "artistic" or more "pleasing and understandable" to Western ears or to provide critical analysis. This most fascinating and valuable research must be left for future consideration.

Much has been written about Arabian music; but nearly always the judgments come from persons of little musical knowledge, whose opinions are founded upon a restricted number of hearings. To the Western ear, first impressions of Arabian music are always unfavorable. "Music of the most barbarous kind,"

"Most revolting to the ear," "One's ears are tortured by the native music," "The braying of an ass is sweeter than their softest note, whether vocal or instrumental"—these comments were heard from Westerners after their first introduction to Arabian music. At first hearing, it is utterly impossible for a Westerner to appreciate this music, which is so little in accord with our own sensations. It is by virtue of a habit acquired, in some degree unknowingly, that one admires today the musical works which were rejected yesterday. Though Arabian music may at first appear harsh and rude, it not infrequently grows upon one who has, so to say, become reconciled to its unpolished exterior sufficiently to catch its true spirit. However strange and unsatisfactory it may appear to the ear unaccustomed to it, Arabian music has great charms for the initiated. The writer, as he came to understand this folk music and art of the Arabian, developed a keener understanding and a finer appreciation for the people themselves.

In order to judge Arabian music, one must understand it, just as one must understand a language in order to appreciate its real beauties.[1] The reader should keep in mind that the present Arabian melodies are comparable to European music of the period preceding the thirteenth century. Arabian music today is no more than the song of the troubadour and minstrel. One must keep an open mind and give the ear an opportunity to become educated. If Arabian music is "foreign" and "exotic" to the Western ear, that is not a just cause for labeling it "impossible," "primitive," "out of tune," or "voluptuous and noisy." Let the reader remember that Arabian music is a music apart, resting on laws entirely different from those which govern our system, and that we must become accustomed to their scales, or rather their modes, putting aside our Western ideas of tonality.

Many of the melodies in this collection—perhaps most of them —were originally not "religious" folk tunes but secular ones.

[1] For the benefit of the reader wishing to study Arabian music, a selected bibliography is given at the end of this book.

Naturally, there is prejudice, especially among Western missionaries in the Near East, against the use of these melodies in the church, because of possible undesirable associations. However, the Arab sings these songs with far greater personal satisfaction, understanding, enthusiasm, joy, and uplift than he does the Western or "foreign" airs imposed upon him. A lack of appreciation of the indigenous music, so close to the hearts of the people, has been disastrous to the whole art and practice of native melody in the church proper.

BLESSED ART THOU, O GOD

Blessed Art Thou, O God!
Teach Me Thy Laws!

BROTHERLY LOVE

1

We are the sons of the merciful Father.
Brothers are we:
We shall all meet in Paradise some day
Happy to be!
Though we may differ in race and in language,
We may be one:
One in the faith in the perfect redemption
Of Jesus, the Son.

2

Jesus the Son was our wonderful pattern,
Loving all men.
We must be like Him in loving our neighbors
As He did then.
Sympathy true for a brother's affliction
Then let us give,
And with a hand that is strong and assuring
Help Him to live.

3

Let us be happy when others are happy,
Weep when they weep:
Working with Christ in his untiring seeking
For the lost sheep.
Just as the branch in the vine will keep growing,
We must abide,
Showing devotion to Jesus and keeping
Close to His side.

CHRISTIAN DUTIES

(*Chorus*)

Lord, who shall abide in Thy tabernacle?
Who shall dwell in Thy holy hill,
In Thy holy hill?

1

He that walketh uprightly, and worketh righteousness,
And speaketh the truth in his heart,
And speaketh the truth in his heart.

2

He that backbiteth not with his tongue,
Nor doeth evil to his neighbor,
Nor taketh up a reproach against his neighbor.

3

In whose eyes a vile person is condemned;
But he honoureth them that fear the Lord.
He that sweareth to his own hurt, and changeth not.

4

He that putteth not out his money to usury,
Nor taketh reward against the innocent.
He that doeth these things shall never be moved.
—Psalm 15

COME TO ME, ALL YE THAT LABOR

Jesus said:
Come to me, all ye that labor!
Take my yoke, all ye that labor!
   I will give you rest:
Rest to all who labor,
Rest to all who labor.
For my yoke is easy,
And my burden light;
   And you will find rest.

DO NOT FORGET ME, O GOD

1

Oh, do not forget me, dear God, my Protector,
A light for my guidance, give me when I pray,
When we ask for Thy grace, O Father of mercy,
From Thy throne Thou wilt answer and give it alway.

(*Chorus*)

My comfort art Thou when deep sorrow o'ertakes me,
When my faith has grown weak and my courage is gone.
Thy smile lights my pathway; the sense of Thy presence
Reminds me again I am never alone.

2

To see Thy sweet face is the thing that I long for,
O Desire of my soul, heal my wounds as I pray.
The source of my gladness, the source of all kindness,
For Thou art my portion, forever and aye.

GIVE ME A CLEAN HEART

1

Give me a clean heart, O generous Father.
Give light to my eyes, the right path to see;
O God, hear my prayer and pity my weakness.
Guide sinners to come with their wounds unto Thee.

2

Thy righteousness precious is what I should follow,
Thy spirit of guidance, my strength for the strife;
O God, be forgiving and lead me to safety.
Then joy shall abide in my heart all my life.

3

O sinners, come taste and drink the clear water
Give thanks unto God and his precepts revere.
Give praise and thanksgiving to God the Eternal,
And know, mind and heart, of His love so sincere.

GOD'S CARE

1

The Father who is in heaven,
Creator of all creation!
I feel His presence always,
He leads me in the darkness.

2

He feeds the birds of the heavens
And joyously they sing to Him!
He clothes the earth with goodness,
With fruit and lovely flowers.

3

He counts all the hairs of my head
And never forgets their number!
Likewise, the thoughts of my heart
Are known to the Eternal.

HOLY, HOLY, HOLY

Holy is God, Holy is the Strong One.
Holy is the One that never dies.
Have mercy on us, have mercy on us.

LITTLE THINGS

1

Little drops of water,
Little grains of sand,
Make the mighty ocean
And the pleasant land.

2

Thus the little minutes,
Humble though they be,
Make the mighty ages,
Of eternity.

3

Thus our little errors
Lead the soul away
From the path of virtue
Far in sin to stray.

4

Little deeds of kindness,
Little words of love,
Make our earth an Eden,
Like the heaven above.

5

Little seeds of mercy
Sown by youthful hands,
Grow to bless the nations
Far in heathen lands.

—JULIA A. FLETCHER CARNEY

THE LORD IS MY SHEPHERD

1

The Lord is my shepherd;
I shall not want.

2

He maketh me to lie down in green pastures:
He leadeth me beside the still waters.

3

He restoreth my soul:
He leadeth me in the paths of righteousness for his name's sake.

4

Yea, though I walk through the valley of the shadow of death, I
    will fear no evil:
For Thou art with me; Thy rod and Thy staff they comfort me.

5

Thou preparest a table before me in the presence of mine ene-
    mies:
Thou anointest my head with oil; my cup runneth over.

6

Surely goodness and mercy shall follow me all the days of my life:
And I will dwell in the house of the Lord for ever.

                               —Psalm 23

NO LOVE LIKE GOD'S LOVE

1

There is no love like the love
Of Him who saved the world;
He who draws us
To God forever!

2

There is no heart like the heart
That loved us to the death.
He feels with us
In all our troubles.

3

There is no eye like the eye
From which nothing is hid.
It watches us
And holds us steady.

4

There is no voice like the voice
That called the multitude.
The sweetest voice
To those who listen.

5

May we listen to that voice
That teaches us the way
To that dear place
Made ready for us.

O SAVIOUR, SAVE US

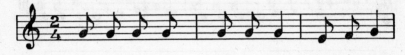

By the intercession
Of the Mother of God,
Jesus, Saviour, save us!

OUR PRAYER

1

Hear my cry, oh, hear my supplication.
From the ends of earth I cry to Thee.
Thy holy name I'll praise forever,
Always on my lips Thy praise will be,
Day by day my vows fulfilling,
Hear my supplication, oh, hear my cry to Thee!

2

Thou art like the highest rock of refuge,
Shelter us from harm throughout our days.
Protect us, guard us from all evil,
Gratefully we sing eternal praise.
Rock of refuge, power of life revealing,
Songs of gratitude we evermore will raise.

PRAISE OUR CREATOR

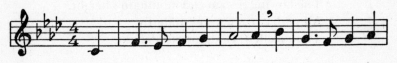

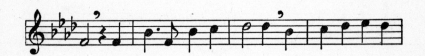

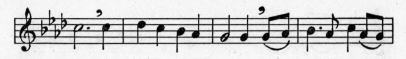

1

All beauty in this world of ours
Of meadow green and forest shade;
All perfect things, so wonderful,
For us, our great Creator made.

2

Praise be to Thee, Almighty One,
For summer's sun and winter's cold,
For all the varied fruits of earth;
Hearts to enjoy, eyes to behold.

3

The days, the nights of stars and dreams,
The flowing stream and mountain's height.
All perfect things, so wonderful,
Thou madest, God, for our delight.

THE PRESENCE OF GOD

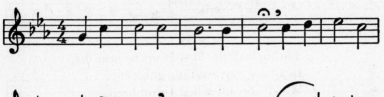
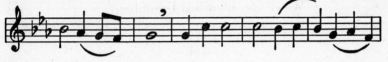

1

O mighty Creator, Thou dost know
The inmost thoughts of all Thy children.
There is nothing hid from Thee,
O God of hosts!

2

Look on me, O Giver of all things,
And lead me, for I belong to Thee!
Openly and in secret
Would I please Thee.

3

Live Thou within my heart, O Father!
Guard every thought and word and action.
In time of sickness, heal me;
Keep Thou my soul.

4

In all my work, be Thou my helper,
Be my companion when I travel;

Help me to see aright,
Supply my needs.

5

Through all the busy hours be near me,
In all my conversation, guide me;
Watch o'er me when I slumber,
Give me sweet rest.

6

Oh, let me feel Thy presence ever,
Be Thou my Helper and my Shield,
Keep me and grant me victory
When death shall call.

REPENTANCE

1

Test me, O God, I pray,
And know my secret thoughts.
Send out Thy light to guide,
Chasten my wayward heart.

2

Make pure, O God, my thoughts
And cleanse my heart's desire;
Forgive, I pray, my sinfulness.
Consider all my works.

3

Lighten the chambers of my soul
Where my rebellion lies.
Teach me, O God, Thy perfect will—
So shall my sins be healed.

4

Be Thou my help and stay
When evil tempts my heart.
Lead me by righteous paths
Unto Thy perfect way.

SONG OF PEACE

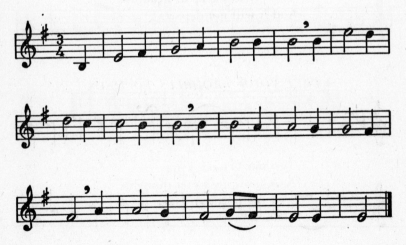

1

Let not your heart be troubled
Nor let it be afraid;
My peace I give unto you,
The peace for which I paid.

2

Our peace is in Jehovah
Peace that shall never cease;
There is no need of asking
The world to give us peace.

3

Our rest is in Jehovah,
Forever will it stay;
It brings delight unending,
Along life's happy way.

4

Our joy is in Jehovah,
And gladness fills the heart;
This joy will keep us steadfast
And it will not depart.

TAKE YOUR TROUBLES TO JESUS

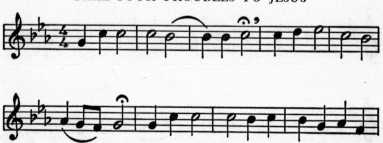

1

The Lord ascended to His throne in heaven,
For us, He ever lives to intercede.
He came to earth and carried heavy burdens,
The sorrows of mankind and all their need.

2

He knows our weaknesses and all our troubles;
He lived on earth and so can understand.
Compassionate is He and knows our longings;
He comforts us and holds us by His hand.

3

Because He was, in truth, a "Man of Sorrows,"
Acquainted, too, with grief of every kind,
With utter confidence we lean upon Him,
And joy unspeakable and peace we find.

THANKS BE TO GOD

1

Thanks be to God whose goodness
Is like a flooding sea;
The earth with rain He waters
That fruitful it may be.

2

For all Thy gifts we thank Thee,
For life and health and food;
For the uncounted riches
Thou givest for our good.

3

Accept, for all Thy goodness,
Dear God, our grateful love;
From hearts that cannot measure
Thy blessings from above.

WHAT SHALL I RENDER UNTO THE LORD?

1

What shall I render unto God
For all His wondrous gifts to me?
His cup of grace I will accept,
His name upon my life shall be.

2

What shall I render unto God?
Obedience to the truth and right:
A life of faithfulness till death
Is ever glorious in His sight.

3

I am a servant unto God
Forever, and a servant's son.
I will give humble sacrifice
And praise His name, His will be done.

WORSHIP THE LORD

1

Almighty Spirit, Thou art God!
Our spirits all are born of Thee.
Thou art the ever present One,
Our heart's intent is Thine to see.

2

No hypocrite will be unknown
Though he may hide with care his skin.
The worshipers God doth accept
Must be sincere and pure within.

3

He may not lift his eyes to heaven
While worldly sins his soul may bear;
The God of peace who judgeth all
Will not accept unworthy prayer.

4

If we would reach to the Divine
We must forsake the downward gaze;
Our lives must follow His design—
Then will He guide in all our ways.

5

Test me, O God, that I may be
Both clean and beautiful in heart:
A faithful worshiper of Thee.
Then speak and tell me, "Blessed thou art."

Benedictus

ALTHOUGH at this writing the reader is well aware of the fact that Palestine as a world nation no longer exists, that the Arab portion of the land has become a part of Greater Jordan while the Jewish area has become Israel, it seemed only correct that the writer record his findings in the Holy Land just prior to the tragic military struggle between Arab and Jew in order to preserve the material, limited as it may be, for future reference and study.

The long established pilgrimages to holy shrines are still undertaken by loyal Christian followers, but not wholly in the traditional fashion here recorded. New national boundary lines, along with religious, racial, and political misunderstandings, have brought about a drastic change in the lives of Holy Land residents. National, district, and village folkways—religious and secular—have accepted alteration out of sheer necessity. Of course youthful acceptance of "modern" ways and increased educational opportunities have also played an important role in the changes brought about.

Folk music is ever changing, new variants blossom like spring flowers after April rains. The recent turn of events in the Holy Land, however, has caused a major revolution in the folk music, art, and dance in that area.

Villages and districts, so recently proud of their distinctive melodies, poems, stories, traditions, art, and dance, have unwittingly experienced a rapid revision of their folkways and general mode of living. Out of necessity, Palestinian areas remaining in Arab hands have accepted and absorbed refugees from now non-Arab lands. Village festivities are no longer attended only by native villagers or clansmen. Folk songs and dances, so naturally a part of Eastern celebrations, have undergone both deliberate and unintentional alteration to best satisfy the needs of the new populace. The best, or at least the most easily adaptable parts of folk dances and songs from participating tribes, have undergone a natural give-and-take change, thus meeting the necessary demands of the new participants.

The religious folk songs and chants herein recorded may never again be heard in popular rendition. Perhaps only among the aged and shut-in, will the variants be lovingly remembered and softly hummed. These melodies, words, and tales, then, may serve well the historian, the musicologist, and the folk specialist in his search for traditional folklore and song of the pre-Israel era.

The transcription and recording of these religious folk songs and the writing of the traditional religious folk rites, for those in search of such information, is undoubtedly its own justification. It is hoped that it may stimulate future interest in the recording and use of religious folk music in Arab lands. It is also hoped, however, that, in the sharing of these intimate and precious experiences, a better understanding and appreciation has been built for the Holy Land Christian Arab.

Bibliography

Bridgeman, Charles T., "Statement Prepared for the Anglo-American Committee of Inquiry on Palestine." Unpublished paper, Trinity Church, 74 Trinity Place, New York, 1946, 20 pp.

Dickinson, Edward, *Music in the History of the Western Church*. New York: Charles Scribner's Sons, 1902.

Hall, Henry Noble, *Why Palestine?* 150 E. 49th St., New York: Author, 1946. 32 pp.

Hitti, Philip K., *The Arabs: A Short History*. Princeton: Princeton University Press, 1949. 224 pp.

———, *History of the Arabs*, 2nd ed., rev. London: Macmillan & Co., 1940. 767 pp.

———, *History of Syria, Including Lebanon and Palestine*. London: Macmillan & Co., 1951. 749 pp.

———, "Palestinian Arabs Descended from Natives Before Abraham," *Papers on Palestine*, No. 1, pp. 16–20. New York: The Institute of Arab American Affairs, 1945.

Hoade, Fr. Eugene, *Guide to the Holy Land*. Jerusalem: Franciscan Press, 1942. 363 pp.

Lang, Paul Henry, *Music in Western Civilization*. New York: W. W. Norton & Co., 1941. 1107 pp.

McKinney, Howard D., and W. R. Anderson, *Music in History*. New York: American Book Co., 1940. 904 pp.

Matson, Olaf G., *The American Colony Palestine Guide*. Jerusalem: The American Colony Stores, 1930. 333 pp.

The New Chain-Reference Bible, compiled and edited by Frank Charles Thompson. Indianapolis: B. B. Kirkbridge Bible Co., 1943. 1563 pp.

The New Testament, Revised Standard Version. New York: Thomas Nelson & Sons, 1946. 553 pp.

Salvador-Daniel, Francesco, *The Music and Musical Instruments of the Arab*. London: William Reeves, 1914. 273 pp.

Wysner, Glora M., "Dilemma in Palestine," *Bulletin*, No. 6, Nov., 1944, Committee on Work Among Moslems. 156 Fifth Ave., New York: Foreign Missions Conference. 8 pp.

ARABIAN MUSIC

SELECTIVE BIBLIOGRAPHY AVAILABLE IN ENGLISH

Farmer, Henry George, *Arabian Influence on Musical Theory*. London: Harold Reeves, 1925. 22 pp.

———, *Arabic Musical Manuscripts in the Bodleian Library*. London: William Reeves, 1925. 18 pp.

———, *Historical Facts for the Arabian Musical Influence*. London: William Reeves, 1930. 376 pp.

———, *History of Arabian Music to the Thirteenth Century*. London: Luzac & Co., 1929. 264 pp.

———, *Influence of Music from Arabic Sources*. London: Harold Reeves, 1926. 29 pp.

———, *Maimonides on Listening to Music*. Bearsden, Scotland: Author, 1941. 21 pp.

———, *Minstrelsy of The Arabian Nights*. Bearsden, Scotland: Author, 1945. 78 pp.

———, *Sa'adyah Gaon on the Influence of Music*. London: Arthur Probsthain, 1943. 109 pp.

———, *Studies in Oriental Musical Instruments,* 2nd Series. Glasgow: The Civic Press, 1939. 98 pp.

———, editor, *Ancient Arabian Musical Instruments*. Glasgow: The Civic Press, 1938. 46 pp.

———, editor and translator, *An Old Moorish Lute Tutor*. Bearsden, Scotland: Editor, 1933. 68 pp.

———, editor and translator, *Music: The Priceless Jewel*. Bearsden, Scotland: Editor, 1942. 27 pp.

———, editor and translator, *Turkish Instruments of Music in the Seventeenth Century*. Glasgow: The Civic Press, 1937. 47 pp.

Hague, Eleanor, and Marion Leffingwell, *Music in Ancient Arabia and Spain* (English version of Julián Ribera, *La Música de las Cantigas*). Stanford: Stanford University Press, 1929. 283 pp.

Hitti, Philip K., *History of the Arabs*. London: Macmillan & Co., 1940. 767 pp.

Salvador-Daniel, Francesco, *The Music and Musical Instruments of the Arab*. London: William Reeves, 1914. 276 pp.

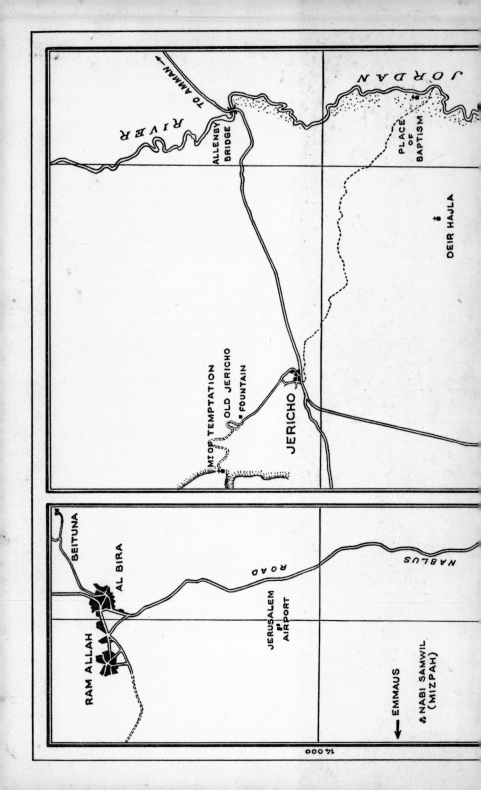